THE LIFE AND RELIGION
OF MOHAMMED

Publisher's Note

Author J.L. Menezes uses an older English spelling of Mohammed. We've chosen to use the contemporary spelling on the cover of our edition.

Other books on the topic offered by
Roman Catholic Books:

Moslems, by Belloc and Oussani, $16.95
Sword of the Prophet, by Serge Trifkovic, $19.95
The Great Divide, by Alvin J. Schmidt, $19.95

And related titles:

The Death of the West, by Patrick J. Buchanan, $25.95
The History of Israel, by Msgr. Giuseppe Ricciotti, Two Volumes, $59.95
History of Europe, by W. Eugene Shiels, SJ, $29.90

THE LIFE AND

RELIGION OF MOHAMMED

THE PROPHET OF ARABIA

REV. J.L. MENEZES

ORIGINALLY PUBLISHED IN 1912

Roman Catholic Books

Post Office Box 255, Harrison, NY 10528
BooksforCatholics.com

ISBN 1-929291-68-X

PREFACE

It is not without much misgiving that I offer this little book to the public. I am sensible of its many defects, and were it not that many friends, who had the kind patience to see my notes on the subject, have strongly recommended their publication, I should hardly have felt the courage to prepare them for the press.

I frankly confess that the contents of this book are not original. They have been compiled from the best and most trustworthy authors, who have written on the subject, and I am especially indebted to the researches of men such as Sale, Bettany, and Stobbart.

I do not think that any important matter connected with Islam or its founder, has been omitted; and in treating of the leading features of Islam and of the life of its prophet, I have sought to state the bare facts without comment, and whilst compromising nothing of the truth, have endeavoured to avoid everything like partisanship or prejudice.

In this modest effort, I have had no other aim, than that of placing before my readers, Mahommed and Islam in their true colours—so that over 60 millions of my countrymen in India, who blindly follow Mahommed as their heaven-sent prophet and leader and adhere to

Islam as the one divinely revealed religion and the only true way of salvation, may open their eyes, and behold how they are deceived, and consequently take the necessary steps towards finding a better leader and a more certain way of salvation.

While exposing the true life of the prophet of Islam, who is held in such deep veneration by his followers, and who is universally admired for many excellent qualities; and while giving some explanatory remarks on the religion taught by him and which is followed by over one-eighth of the population of the world, I regret the unpleasant necessity of recording certain details of his life, and of passing certain strictures on his religion, which will not prove pleasant reading to his followers and admirers. But facts are facts, and in recording them, I have simply followed the authors from whom I have taken the contents of this book. In doing so, I utterly disclaim the intention of offering any insult to the great prophet of Islam, or any offence to his followers; or of vilifying the religion he has taught. And while vindicating the truth of the facts, I have done my best to observe the golden rule of Christian charity.

Finally, since my chief aim has been a popular exposition of the subject, I have not aimed at style or at literary perfection. I am conscious of many repetitions of the same ideas, and of many defects both in language and mode of expression; And therefore I earnestly request both Mahommedan readers and other critics to extend to me their indulgence and forbearance.

I cannot conclude this Preface without expressing my grateful acknowledgments to many kind friends who have rendered help or have shown interest in this compilation.

In a particular manner I must record my deep sense of gratitude to the RT. REV. DR. A. CAVADINI, S.J., who

was the first to encourage and help me in this work—
To his sacred memory and to that of his predecessor
the RT. REV. DR. N. PAGANI, S.J. the two first great
bishops of Mangalore, in token of my deep love, veneration and gratitude I respectfully *dedicate* this book.

Mangalore,   J. L. MENEZES
Patronage of St Joseph
17th April, 1911.

CONTENTS

MAHOMMED
THE PROPHET OF ARABIA

PART FIRST

THE LIFE OF MAHOMMED

ARABIA AND ITS INHABITANTS

ARABIA, commonly called Arbistan, famous as the birth-place of Mahommed, the founder of a religion which is now professed by about one eighth of the earth's population, is a large tract of land bounded by the river Euphrates, the Persian Gulf, the Sindian, Indian and Red Seas and part of the Mediterranean Sea. Arabia Proper however is much narrower, reaching no further northward than the Isthmus which runs from Aila to the head of the Persian Gulf, and is bounded on the north by Asiatic Turkey, on the east by the Persian Gulf, on the south by the Arabian Sea and on the west by the Red Sea.

Arabia Proper was formerly divided into (1) Arabia Petraea, or rocky Arabia, which included the whole north western portion, (2) Arabia Felix, or happy Arabia, comprising the west and south-western coasts of Arabia, and (3) Arabia Deserta comprising the whole interior. Modern geographers however generally divide it into

A   1

seven provinces namely (1) The Sinai Desert, (2) The
Hedjaz or the Land of Pilgrimage, (3) Yaman, (4) Hadramaut, (5) Oman, or the kingdom of Muscat, (6) Bahrein
or the province situated along the Persian Gulf, (7) Nezd,
or the central highlands of Arabia. Some writers on
the other hand reduce them all to two provinces,
namely Yaman and Hedjaz.

The province of Yaman which extends along the
Indian Ocean and part of the Red Sea on the south
and west sides, has been famous from all antiquity
for the excellence of its climate, the verdure and
fertility of its soil and the greatness of its wealth,
which induced Alexander the Great to form a design
of conquering it and fixing there his royal seat.
The charm and fertility of this province are due to
its mountains which being well watered, make the
valleys very fertile, and the many springs which flow
from them make the country very delightful. The
province of Yaman is subdivided into several smaller
provinces as Hadramaut, Oman, Shihr, Nazran etc. of
which Shihr is famous for its frankincense.

The province of Hadjaz or the Land of Pilgrimage,
which is situated on the north of Yaman, and which
includes in it the lesser provinces of Tehama, Najd,
and Yamama, derives its celebrity from its two chief
cities, namely Mecca, meaning a place of great concourse,
celebrated for its famous temple and as the birthplace
of Mahommed, and Medina for being the place of
Mahommed's residence and of his interment. Mecca is
certainly one of the most ancient cities in the world ;
it is seated in a stony and barren valley, surrounded
on all sides with mountains.

The Arabians, the inhabitants of this spacious country,
are divided into two classes, namely the Ancient and the
Modern Arabians. The former were very numerous,
and were divided into several tribes, the most famous

of which were Ad, Thamud, Jadis, Tasm, Jorham, and
Amalek. The tribe of Ad was descended from Ad, the
son of Aws or Us, the son of Aram, the son of Sem, the
son of Noah, who after the confusion of tongues, settled
in Hadramaut, a sub-province of Yaman, where his
posterity greatly multiplied. The tribe of Thamud
was the posterity of Thamud the son of Gather, the son
of Aram; this tribe first dwelt in Yaman, but being
expelled from this place, retired and settled down in
the province of Hedjaz.

The tribe of Tasm descended from Lud the son of
Sem and that of Jadis descended from Gather, dwelt
together for some time under the government of Tasm,
but internal feuds led to their destruction. The tribe
of Jorham, whose ancestor, some pretend, was one of the
eighty persons saved in the Ark of Noah according
to a Mahomadan tradition, was contemporary with Ad,
and soon utterly perished.

The tribe of Amalek, descended from Amalek the son
of Eliphaz the son of Esau, became very powerful, and in
the course of time they conquered Egypt under their
chief, by name Walid, the first who took the name of
Pharaoh. All these tribes of Ancient Arabians ultimately
were either destroyed by internal strifes or merged into
other tribes.

The Modern Arabians are sprung from two stocks,
namely from Joktan or Kahtan, the son of Eber mentioned in Genesis (x. 26) and the other from Adnan,
descended from Ismael the son of Abraham by Hagar,
an Egyptian slave. The descendants of Joktam call
themselves Al Arab al Ariba that is pure Arabs, while
the prosterity of Adnan are called Al Arab al Mosterba,
that is naturalised or mixed Arabs, because the prosterity
of Ismael have no claim to be called pure Arabs as their
ancestor both by origin and language was an Hebrew.
The Arabs may be divided into two classes, namely

those who *wander* and are called *Bedouins* or dwellers
in tents in the desert; and those who are *settled*, that
is who live in cities and towns. The former employed
themselves in pasturage and also in pillaging of
passengers, changing their habitation as the con-
venience of water and of pasturage for their cattle
invited them; the latter on the other hand lived by the
cultivation of land and by the exercise of all sorts of
trade, they were very good merchants and navigators
and were thus continually engaged themselves in
commerce with the ports on the coast on the opposite
shores of Africa, and with Persia or India.

The Arabians were for centuries governed by the
descendants of Joktan, who peopled the south-west of
Arabia. Yarab one of the sons of Joktan founded
the kingdom of Yaman, in which was included also the
kingdom of Sheba, whose queen afterwards visited
King Solomon. The kingdom of Yaman was the most
powerful state in all Arabia. The country itself is
superior in many respects to most other parts of Arabia.

The Arabs of Yaman dwelt in towns and cultivated
the soil. Taiz Yerim, Cana and Hodeidah are some of
its chief towns. In Yaman there are two rainy seasons,
in spring and in autumn, so there is generally an
abundance of water in the numerous reservoirs stored
for irrigation. The soil is extraordinarily fertile and
the people are very industrious. However in early days
the greatness of these people was chiefly in their traffic;
they were the only navigators who dared to cross the
seas to India and to the east, and their trade with India
and the east brought to them immense wealth, which
made them very powerful. Jorahan another son of
Joktan founded the kingdom of Hedjaz, which thereafter
became the most important in all Arabia for its possession of the holy places of Mecca and Medina, and is
called the Holy Land of Arabia.

The Arabs, situated as they were between the great
populations of Asia and Africa, naturally possessed many
religious features in common with the adjacent peoples.
The Arabs originally acknowledged the existence of one
supreme God, creator of the universe, whom they called
Allah Taala, the most high God.

Their religion soon lost its earliest monotheism, and
degenerated into gross idolatry, fetichism, animal
worship and star worship.   They first of all adopted
Sabeanism or the worship of the hosts of heaven.
Observing how changes of the weather happened at
the rising and the setting of certain stars, they began
to ascribe divine power to these stars and to worship
them as gods.   It is said that the ancient Arabs had
seven celebrated temples dedicated to the seven planets.
Very soon, however, the star worship became greatly
corrupted and other deities, superstitious and idolatrous
practices, were introduced.   Ancient Arabia was a
refuge for all sorts of religious fugitives and each band
added something new to the national stock of religious
ideas.   From their pagan neighbours, they adopted the
doctrine of the abodes or haunts of gods ; marked
them out as sacred territories by pillars, and
within which bloodshed, cutting of trees, and
killing game was forbidden, and within such en-
closures the blood of sacrifices was smeared on sacred
stones, and gifts were hung up on the trees.   This is
the origin of the Haramain or sacred territory around
Mecca and Medina.   Everywhere in Arabia there were
wells, pillars and heaps of stones, where the Arab
devotees congregated to obtain special blessings.
Sacrifices were common, but not by fire.   The blood
of the sacrifices was smeared over the rude stone altars,
and the flesh was eaten by the worshipper.   First
fruits were given to the gods, and libations were
poured out.   They also worshipped idols, ten of whom

are mentioned by name in the Koran ; the most famous
among these however are Al-Lat, the chief goddess;
this was the chief idol of the tribe of Thakif at Taif,
who tried to compromise with Mahommed to accept
Islam, if he would not destroy their god Al-Lat for
three years ; *Al Uzza* identified with planet Venus, and
worshipped at times under the form of an acacia tree ;
and *Manat* a huge stone worshipped as an altar by
several tribes. The Arabs also worshipped angels,
whom they call female gods and the daughters of God.
They made their images and paid them divine worship,
because they imagined that these images of angels
were animated by them and were intercessors with God
for man. The most celebrated and central object of
Arab worship however was the *blackstone* of Mecca, set
in the corner of a square building called the Kaaba, in
which also are placed the images of Abraham and
Ismael each carrying in their hands divine arrows.
According to the tradition among the early Arabians,
the story runs that when God expelled Adam and Eve
after their sin of disobedience, from paradise, Adam
landed on a mountain in Ceylon and Eve fell at Jiddah
on the western coast of Arabia, and after a hundred
years of wandering Adam met his wife at Mecca, and
here Adam, according to the instruction and design
given by Allah constructed a tabernacle on the site of
the present Kaaba, and he put in its foundation the
famous stone, which they say, had also fallen from
paradise when the primal pair fell, and which was
once whiter than milk, but since turned black on
account of the sins of the pilgrims who touched it.
Further they say that Mecca stands on a spot exactly
beneath God's throne in heaven. The present Kaaba,
they say, was built by Abraham and his son Ismael
and the black stone which had been missing, was
shewn to Ismael by the angel Gabriel, and it

was used as a corner stone for the building of the
Kaaba.

The Persians likewise had by their proximity and
frequent intercourse with the Arabians, introduced the
Magian religion among some of the Arab tribes. The
Jews who had fled in great numbers into Arabia from
the fearful destruction of their country by the Romans,
had also introduced the Jewish religion among several
of the tribes. Christianity likewise had made great
progress among this nation before the birth of
Mahommed ; several tribes had already embraced the
Christian faith. The Christians of the Jacobite and
of the Nestorian sects were also numerous in Arabia.
The desert of Arabia was by this time peopled with
many ascetic anchorites, whose perfect retirement from
the world, whose consecration of their lives to austerities
and pious practices, and whose steadfast preparation for
the life to come had likewise greatly impressed the
minds of these Arabs. The multiplicity and variety
of so many religions and religious ideas and practices
not infrequently conflicting with one another had
already produced in the minds of these people the
necessity of finding a religion that would be
re-conciliatory, and that could be adapted to the
nature of the people and thus the path was laid open
to the new religion called Hanifs, which was introduced
just before the birth of Mahommed. These Hanifs
were a small number of Arabs, who worshipped only
Allah, rejecting polytheism, and sought freedom from
sin and resignation to God's will. Thus we see
Hanifism was only a step to Islam, and such was the
state of religion in Arabia before the time of Mahommed,
called by him 'the time of ignorance,' and thus to a
very great extent the ground was prepared for the
prophet of Islam.

THE Arabs had enjoyed for several thousand years an almost absolute freedom from foreign dominion or occupation. Neither the Egyptians, the Assyrians, the Babylonians, the ancient Persians, nor the Macedonians in their march of conquest ever subjugated or held any part of Arabia. But at the beginning of the Christian era, the proud Arabs were compelled to bend their necks repeatedly to the yoke of Roman, Abyssinian and Persian rulers. Roman domination invaded even Mecca itself and the Emperor Heraclius, it is said, nominated Othman, then a convert to Christianity, as governor of Mecca. However, just before the time of the coming of the Prophet of Mecca, the political state of the world was quite changed, and was in a very disturbed condition. After the death of the Emperor Constantine, the Roman empire had greatly declined, being in great part overrun by the Goths and Huns. The Persian empire had likewise declined on account of internal broils and dissensions occasioned by the preaching of Mazdak, who, pretending to be a Prophet sent from God, was spreading a doctrine of a very low moral tone which would have totally ruined the empire, had not he with his followers been put to death by the Persian emperor Anushirwan.

About this time another pretended Prophet, Manes the founder of the Manicheans, had succeeded to some extent by his new doctrine in restoring the ancient Magian religion in Persia. The Abyssinian wars and internal dissensions during the century preceding Mahommed had reduced that empire to a very weak state. Thus while these empires were growing weak and declining, Arabia began to acquire great strength by the immigration of crowds of refugees, who had fled

from the tyranny of Greeks and Romans, as well as by
the influx of those people who had escaped from the
violent proceedings of the domineering tribes and sects,
whose attrocities during these continual dissensions and
feuds had forced the weak to seek refuge in a free
country, as Arabia then was. The different tribes of
Arabia were greatly divided among themselves, and
were independent of each other, and the influx of these
immigrants seeking refuge and shelter had greatly
increased the strength of several of these tribes. Arabia
thus at the time of the advent of Mahommed had become
the centre of many political schemes and plots, and the
whole peninsula was awake to the touch of the Romans,
Abyssinians and Persians, who had overrun the country
and had held it under their sway, and hence these tribes
were now ready to rally around any banner that led to
a national deliverance. This state of things greatly
aided the progress of Mahommedanism; for it would
have been scarcely possible to establish and propagate
the new religion, had the Arabs been united into one
social and civil power. Thus the state of affairs, both
religious and political, greatly prepared the way for
Mahommed's extraordinary success.

BIRTH OF MAHOMMED AND HIS EARLY LIFE

ISHMAEL the son of Abraham by Hagar, born about
1910 B.C. had married a daughter of Modadh, the
Jorhamite chief of Mecca, and from this marriage he
had twelve sons, the forefathers of the so-called al
Arab al Mostareba, *i.e.* naturalised Arabs. From them
descended Adnan 130 B.C., the father of Maadd the
ancestor of the Maadite tribe from whom the Koreish
tribes descended. From Maadd in the seventh genera-
tion descended Nadhr A.D. 134 the father of Malik,
the father of Fihr Koreish A.D. 200.

About this time the Jorhamite chiefs had succeeded
in assuming the supremacy of the whole of Hajaz
province and had even usurped the privileges* of
the Kaaba, which rightly belonged to the lineal
descendants of Ishmael. The Jorhamites retained their
power both over Mecca and the Kaaba for a very long
time, until it was wrested from them by Khozaates
who also retained the power until it was finally wrested
from them by the adventurous Kussai, a true Ishmaelite,
being the sixth in lineal descent from Fehr Koreish.
This Kussai had married Hobba the daughter of
Holeil the Khozaaite king, and on the death of Holeil,
Kussai with the support of the other Koreish families
set about to assert and to defend the right of his family
to the guardianship of the Kaaba and the government
of Mecca. This leader was born about 400 A.D. and
having succeeded over the supremacy of Hajaz and
having obtained the guardianship of the Kaaba, the
most sacred object and the holiest place of the Arab
worship and also the government of Mecca, he gathered
together and brought down to the Valley many of his
tribes, who had previously lived on the hills. He laid
out the town anew and allotted quarters therein to each
family. Kussai held the keys of the Kaaba and it was
his office to provide the pilgrims with food and drink.
Thus even before the time of Mahommed, the Kaaba
was the object of frequent pilgrimages, during which
the worshipping and kissing of the black stone took
place, as well as the practice of making the seven
circuits round the sacred edifice.

* The privileges of the Kaaba were five. (1) The Hijaba *i.e.*
possessing the keys and the control of the Kaaba. (2) The
'Sicaya' and the 'Rifada,' *i.e.* the right of providing drink and
food for the pilgrims. (3) The 'Kiyada' the command of the
troops in war. (4) The 'Liwa' *i.e.* the right of affixing the
banner to the staff and of presenting it to the standard bearer.
(5) The 'Dar Ul Nadwa' *i.e.* the presidency of the Hall of Council.

At Mecca, descended from the Koreish tribe and fifth in descent from Kussai, Mahommed was born in the autumn of the year 570 A.D. His father Abdullah was the youngest son of Abdul Muttalib the great-grandson of Kussai, and at that time the chief of the tribe of Koreish. His mother's name was Amina, daughter of Wahib who was descended from Zohra, the first cousin of Kussai. While out on a trading expedition, Abdullah died at Medina, a short time before the birth of this his famous son. When the news of the birth of the child was brought to Abdul Muttalib the grandfather of the child, he went to the house of Amina, took the child in his arms, and giving thanks to God, conferred on it the name of 'Mahommed' or the 'Praised One.' It was then the custom for Koreishite mothers to give their infants to be nursed by Bedouins, who dwelt near the deserts of Arabia, so as to secure for their infants the healthy air of the desert; moreover, grief is said to have dried up the fountain of the mother's breast, and Mahommed was thus for a double reason entrusted to the care of a Bedouin nurse, by name Halima, of the Beni Saad tribe, who took charge of the child for five years. When approaching his fifth year, he appears to have become subject to certain epileptic fits, which alarmed his foster-parent, as such attacks were attributed to the influence of evil spirits and made her resolve to rid herself of the charge, and so he was restored to Amina his mother when he had reached his fifth year. Mahommed long retained a grateful recollection of Halima's care. At the age of six he was taken (575 A.D.) by his mother to Medina. But on the return journey she died and Mahommed was left an orphan in straitened circumstances. The faithful slave Baraka escorted him to Mecca to his grandfather's house, and Abdul Muttalib was consequently obliged to take care of his grandchild during his own life, and at his death (578 A.D.) he enjoined his eldest son Abu Talib, who was brother to Abdullah by the same mother, to provide for the child's future, which Abu Talib very affectionately promised to do, and from that time Abu Talib took great care of this his nephew and trained him up in his own profession as a merchant, and in the year 582 he took him, when yet only twelve years old, on a trading expedition with a caravan into Syria. Thus while under the shelter and favour of Abdul Muttalib the chief man of the Koreish and of his son Abu Talib a man of great mercantile abilities, this pet boy learned what it was to be lordly and to exercise power and never forgot it. Further, the daily association with the ceremonies of the holy house, the superstitious awe which surrounded the place, the prostrations, the prayers, and the pious offerings of the faithful at the Kaaba, his own near relationship to the priestly families, the order and decorum of the house of Abu Talib, where the sacred rites were rigidly observed, made no doubt a strong and lasting impression on his mind. It may be noted here that even before the promulgation of the Moslem doctrines, fasting and prayer had a foremost place amongst Arabs, who had three principal fasts within a year, one of seven, one of nine, and one of thirty days. They prayed three times a day, at sunrise, at noon, and about sunset, turning their faces in the direction of the Kaaba, which was their Kibla, or point of adoration, which all gave that tendency to his thoughts which manifested itself in the prophetic character he afterwards assumed. The youth of Mahommed passed without any other incidents of special interest, except that when he was not engaged in trading expeditions, he employed his time, like other lads of his age, in tending the sheep and goats on the neighbouring hills; and in after years he retained a pleasant recollection of this fact, saying that 'no prophet has been raised up, who has not first done the work of a shepherd.' A few years later, when he was 20 years old, he was perforce engaged in the so-called 'sacrilegious war' between the Koreish and the Hawagin tribes which occurred within the sacred months and was carried on in the sacred territory. 'In this war' Mahommed used to say, 'I discharged arrows at the enemy and I do not regret it.'

MAHOMMED AND KHADIJA

At the age of twenty-five, Mahommed, at the recommendation of his uncle Abu Talib, entered the services of Khadija a noble and rich widow of Mecca who was also a descendant of Kussai ; and in charge of a trading caravan belonging to her, he travelled to Bostra, sixty miles east of the Jordan on the road to Damascus. Leading the caravan to the north, by judicious barter with the Syrian merchants of Bostra, Alleppo and Damascus, he succeeded in doubling Khadija's venture, and on the journey back was prompt to announce to his expectant mistress the success of the caravan that had been led by him. Khadija, highly pleased at the success achieved by the caravan led by Mahommed, and fascinated with his attractive personal qualities and beautiful countenance, intimated her desire of marriage with him, though she was then forty years old and had been already twice married. This marriage proved a very fortunate event for Mahommed, for it raised him to an equality with the richest in Mecca; besides, this lady, possessed of a strong mind and mature experience, was able to maintain a decided ascendency over her husband and to manage him with great wisdom and firmness, and this appears from nothing more strikingly than from the very remarkable fact, that she succeeded

in keeping him from marrying any other wife as long as
she lived, though after her death, when he had long
ceased to be a young man, he indulged without restraint
in the multiplication of wives.   Khadija bore him two
sons, who died young, and four daughters, Zeinale,
Rockeya, Kolthum and Fatima; of whom the most
famous was Fatima.

Mahommed's life, previous to the announcement of
his mission as prophet of Islam, was passed among a
people, with whom, as we have already seen, revenge
was a religious duty, and blood feuds were common,
whole tribes sometimes being involved in them.   Female
infanticide prevailed greatly in many parts of Arabia,
due first to famine and poverty and afterwards as a
social custom to limit the growth of population, because
wars and feuds were tending continually to exceed
females over males.   Further, women in general were
mere chattels, though their rights were respected and
the burying of women alive with a veil was unknown in
Arabia before this horrible custom was introduced later
on by Mahommed.   Polyandry and Polygamy were both
greatly practised and the right of divorce belonged to
the wife as well as to the husband; temporary marriages
were also common, so much so, a marriage was quickly
made and equally with no difficulty was dissolved.
Further idolatry, divination, bloody sacrifices, and
sensualism were greatly prevalent.   As to how far
Mahommed himself conformed to these abominable
beliefs and practices, we have no record, but it may be
well conceived, judging from his later life, that his
inward life gradually revolted from many of these
practices, and that he pondered seriously over the various
ideas and notions he had acquired in his travels as a
merchant regarding the various religious systems and
practices prevailing in the many countries through
which he had travelled.   As Khadija herself was favour-

ably disposed toward Hanifism, it is highly probable that she exercised her commanding influence ever her husband in such a manner as to promote and strengthen his own attachment to that reformatory sect of mono-theists. Further, Mahommed trusted her implicitly, and Khadija yielded to him her whole faith, so that when the world called him impostor and cheat, she was the first to acknowledge him to be indeed the Apostle of God.

MAHOMMED AND KAABA

MAHOMMED possessed an aptitude and tact for forming warm friendships, for shewing gratitude and kindness, and for exercising prudent judgment. When he was about thirty-five years old, the Kaaba at Mecca was rendered insecure by a flood and it was decided to rebuild the walls and cover them with a roof. During the rebuilding of the walls, a dispute arose among the leading families of Mecca as to who should have the honour and privilege of carrying and placing the sacred black stone in its proper place in the new walls. The dispute grew hot and bloodshed was imminent, when it was decided to refer the solution of the dispute to him who first entered the sacred enclosure by the gate of the Beni-Sheyba; when lo! Mahommed was seen ap-proaching and was the first to reach the appointed spot. Thus Mahommed was chosen to decide the question in dispute and he, highly pleased at the fortune thus opened to him and at the same time desirous to please all the chief tribes, took off his mantle and placed the sacred stone on it and said, ' Now let one from each of your four divisions come forward and raise a corner of this mantle,' and this being done Mahommed, by his own hand guided the stone to its place; this prudent decision increased his influence and popularity among

his fellow-tribesmen.   This incident afterwards served
to confirm his own belief in the divineness of his mission
and to strengthen his claim on the faith of his adherents
in after days.   About this time, to make up for the loss
of his own two sons, Mahommed is said to have adopted
his cousin Ali, son of his uncle and protector Abu Talib,
then about six years old, and to have admitted to a
similar relationship, one, Zeid, a slave who had been
presented to him by his wife Khadija.

MAHOMMED AN ANCHORITE

THOUGH after his marriage with Khadija, he still
continued his commercial pursuits and at times
accompanied the yearly caravans north and south, yet
he had ample leisure for that religious meditation to
which he was naturally inclined.   The general tendency
of his mind in this direction, fostered by his early train-
ing and associations in the house of Abu Muttalib and
Abu Talib, inclined him to speculation in matters of
faith and this was further stimulated by the sight of the
gross idolatry, which he saw practised even at the holy
sanctuary of Kaaba, as contrasted with the more
spiritual and holier worship of the Christians and of
the Jews, of which he had been a witness on his visits
to Syria.   From the general spirit of inquiry which
was actuating him ; from the knowledge he had gained
by actual intercourse with those Christians and Jews
who had been instructed in a better faith, however im-
perfect and ill-informed they may have been, and from
dim traditions of the purer faith of their ancestor
Abraham, he gradually became sensible how much such
pure adoration was at variance with the gross and
degrading idolatry and evil practices then prevalent
in Arabia and it is scarcely to be marvelled at, that the
necessity for some reformation occurred to him by which,

freeing the religion from all idolatrous practices, it might be reduced to its original purity.

He was now in his fortieth year and with a brooding anxiety for something that would answer the secret longings of his soul he began often to retire into solitary places and among rocks near Mecca. His favourite resort was a cave at the foot of Mount Hira about three miles from Mecca, and amongst such dark and wild surroundings his mind was wrought up to rhapsodic enthusiasm ; and in this solitary place he conceived the scheme of establishing a new religion or rather as he expressed it of replanting the only true and ancient one professed by Adam, Noah, Abraham, Moses, Jesus and all the prophets, by destroying the gross idolatry into which the generality of his countrymen had fallen and weeding out the corruptions and superstitions which the later Jews and Christians had, as he imagined, introduced into their religion ; and of restoring it to its original purity, which consisted chiefly in the worship of only one God. It may well be that some of the earliest chapters in the Koran date from this time.

Whether this was the effect of an enthusiastic and eccentric mind or only an ambitious design to raise himself to the supreme goverment of his country and a means to satisfy his own sensuality, I will not pretend to determine here ; the subsequent proceedings of his life will shew it abundantly.

During this period of his life, he would sometimes communicate his thoughts and his rhapsodic utterances to the members of his family and to his intimate friends, who already had begun to regard him as a very pious and saintly man, and who were often used to talk among themselves that as Jews and Christians had their prophets and better religions ; so if a prophet should rise among their own tribes, they would most willingly follow his lead and embrace his religious

B

doctrines and would be as devout and holy in their worship of the one true God as the Jews and Christians were.   Such flattering expressions from his own people combined with his own contemplations and designs led him more and more to the persuasion that a preacher or prophet was needed by his people, and he considered why should he not himself step forward as the long desired and destined prophet.   It is scarce to be doubted that Mahommed had a vehement desire to be reckoned as an extraordinary person and this his object he could attain by no means so effectually as by pretending himself to be the messenger sent from God to inform mankind of His Holy will and to bring man to the right path and to the true knowledge of God.

Whatever his motives were, Mahommed was certainly endowed with the personal qualifications which were necessary to enable him to accomplish this his grand project; he was a man of attractive personal qualities with a beautiful countenance, he had an acute and piercing wit and was thoroughly versed in all the arts of insinuation, he was further a man of excellent judgment and well accomplished in business; he was also endowed with a very good memory, and all these natural gifts and qualifications were improved very much by the wide experience and knowledge of men he had acquired by continual observation in his travels.   Further he is described in tradition as a man above middle height, of spare figure, commanding appearance, massive head, noble brow, and jet-black hair.   His eyes were piercing.   He had a long bushy beard.   Decision marked his every movement and he always walked rapidly.   He had the genius to command and expected obedience from equals as well as inferiors. He was a very agreeable man of few words, of an equable cheerful temper, pleasant and familiar in conversation, of inoffensive behaviour towards his

friends and of great condescension towards his inferiors.

As to acquired learning, it is affirmed that he had
none at all, having had no other higher education
than what was customary in his tribe. This defect
was far from being prejudicial or putting a stop to
his design; he and his followers made the greatest
use of it, insisting that the writings which he produced
as revelations from God, could not possibly be a forgery
of his own, because it was not conceivable that a person
who had no education, should be able to compose a
book of such excellent doctrine and in so elegant a
style; and for this reason his followers instead of
being ashamed of their master's ignorance glory in
it as an evident proof of his divine mission.

MAHOMMED AND HIS REVELATIONS

Before outlining the scheme of the religion Mahommed
framed, and the artful contrivances he adopted for its
propagation, we shall briefly narrate the steps he
took towards the achievement of his enterprise and
the circumstances which helped its marvellous success.

Before he made any attempt abroad to begin with
his work of proselytism, he rightly judged that it
was necessary for him to start it by gaining over to
his own religious opinion the inmates of his own
household. He therefore retired with his family
during the month of Ramadan, as he had done several
times before, to the famous cave on mount Hira, and
there after spending some time in pious exercises and
meditations, he discreetly announced the secret of his
mission to his wife Khadija and revealed to her that
the angel Gabriel had just then appeared to him and
once again had told him that he had been appointed
the 'Apostle of God'; he likewise repeated to her

a passage which, he pretended, had been revealed
to him by the the ministry of the same angel.

Khadija who as we have already seen was a believer in Hanifism, received this news with great joy
and communicated it to her cousin Warakah Ebu
Nowfal, who was a Christian and who could write
Hebrew well and was tolerably well versed in the
knowledge of the Christian and Jewish Scriptures;
he readily believed all that Khadija had informed
him and expressed the view that as in former times
the angel Gabriel had been sent by God to make
revelations to Moses and other great prophets; in like
manner he was now sent by God to Mahommed. It
is very probable that Mahommed derived much of his
knowledge of the Christian and Jewish Scriptures,
as well as of many of the Mishna and Talmud
traditions from this man, as well as from one Othman
Ibu-Huweirith, a cousin of Khadija who had long
before embraced Christianity at Constantinople. This
first overture of Mahommed which was attended with
such marked success, and which was made in the
month of Ramadan in the fortieth year of his age, is
generally considered as the outset of his embassy from
heaven and is therefore called the first year of his
mission.

From that time the so-called revelations began to
follow one after another in rapid succession; it is
said that during the moments of these revelations or
inspirations, it was a painful sight to behold the
nervousness of his features, the distortion of his
countenance and the anxiety of mind portrayed on
his face. He would sometimes fall to the ground
like one intoxicated and even on the coldest day his
forehead would be bedewed with sweat. The times
or periods of such occurrences were unexpected even
by Mahommed himself. How far during this time he

was overpowered by hysterical hallucinations, it would
be idle to attempt to determine ; but his epileptic fits
which he had in his young days, now greatly increased
during these his spiritual struggles on account of his
mental excitements and night watchings. He made
use of this natural infirmity with great sagacity to
convince people that at such times he was favoured
with heavenly inspirations and revelations from God.

THE FIRST CONVERTS OF MAHOMMED

WE have already seen how he had succeeded in inducing
his wife Khadija to believe in her husband's apostolic
mission and to follow his doctrine ; he next induced
others who were living under his own roof to do the
same, thus his adopted son and cousin, Ali the son of
Abu Talib and his servant Zeid whom he had adopted
as son, as we have seen above, were made the first
proselytes of the new religion. The next person
Mahommed applied to was his intimate friend Abu
Bekr, a rich merchant and a man of great authority
among the Koreish and one who would be of very great
service to him to forward his enterprise. Abu Bekr
was easily persuaded to believe in the apostolic mission
of Mahommed and to become his disciple. He was
about the same age as Mahommed and his firm attachment to Mahommed gained him the name of 'Al-Sadiq,
or The True'; he is also called 'the Father of the
Virgin,' because his daughter Ayesha was the only
virgin bride of the prophet. Mahommed encouraged
by the conversion of Abu Bekr next prevailed upon
Othman, Abdul Rahman, Saad, Zobeir and Telha, all
chief men living in Mecca, to follow the example of
Abu Bekr. These were the six chief companions who
with a few more were thus converted to Mahommedanism in the space of the first three years of his apostolate.

MAHOMMED PROCLAIMS HIMSELF PROPHET OF ISLAM

ENCOURAGED by so good a beginning, Mahommed kept
his mission no longer a secret; but naming his religion
'Islam' that is 'Surrender to the will of God,' gave out
that God had commanded him to admonish his near
relations of this fact; and with a view to make a greater
impression upon the minds of his relatives about his
divine mission and thus to ensure greater success to
his enterprise, he directed his cousin Ali to prepare a
grand entertainment and to invite to it all his near
relatives, with the object of opening his mind to them,
when they were all gathered together, and thus of
solemnly proclaiming himself as the prophet of God
and their spiritual leader. About forty of his relatives
complied with the invitation and attended the entertainment. Mahommed availing himself of this fairly
large gathering made the following speech to the
assembly during the entertainment—'I know no man
in all Arabia who can offer his kindred a more excellent
thing than I now do you, I offer you happiness both in
life and in that which is to come; God the Almighty
has commanded me to call unto Him you, who therefore will henceforth be assisting me in this noble work
and become my brethren and whom I shall appoint as
my vicegerents.' Mahommed at the close of his speech
which he had made with all unction and fervour, was
quite disappointed, when he saw the whole assembly
ridicule what he had uttered, and every one of them
refused to accept him as their spiritual guide. At this
juncture Ali the beloved adopted son of the prophet
stepped forward and declared very enthusiastically that
not only did he believe Mahommed to be the prophet of
God, but that he offered himself and his services to the
good pleasure of the prophet; whereupon Mahommed
embraced him with great demonstrations of affection,

and desired all who were present to hearken to and to obey Ali as his vicegerent, at which the whole assembly rose up and with loud contemptuous laughter dispersed and returned to their homes conceiving a great dislike and hatred to Mahommed.

MAHOMMED AND THE KOREISH TRIBES

THIS unexpected repulse, however, did not in the least discourage Mahommed, who now began to preach in public at Mecca to the people, who, being attracted with the novelty of his preaching listened to him with some attention and patience, but no sooner did they find him upbraid them and talk contemptuously about their idolatrous worship and accuse them of obstinacy and perverseness, than they were highly provoked and began to despise him, and they declared themselves his enemies, and would soon have procured his ruin, had he not been protected by his uncle Abu Talib, who did his best to pacify the people. Some of the Meccans however, seeing that such men as Abu Bekr, Othman, etc., had quickly become disciples of Mahommed, followed their example and embraced Islam. The Koreish when they saw on one hand Mahommed load them with insults and abuses * and on the other

* Mahommed in Sura 74 uses curses as a revelation from God, against one Walid-ibn-al-Magheira, a chief man among the Koreish, as 'He is an adversary to our signs, I will afflict him with grievous calamities; May he be cursed' . . . again 'may he be cursed, he was elated with pride, and he said this is no other than a piece of magic . . . I will cast him to be bound in hell.' Mahommed treats his uncle Abu-Lahab with similar curses for the bitter hostility with which he opposed the prophet; thus 'Let the hands of Abu Lahab perish and he shall perish. . . . He shall go down to be burned into flaming fire, and his wife also bearing wood, having on her neck a cord of twisted fibres of a palm tree ' (Sura cxi.)
Another specimen of curses, supposed against the same Magheira (Sura lxviii, 11-16) ' Obey not any who is a common

hand, a good many people among the Meccans quietly
follow him, warmly solicited Abu Talib either to
make his nephew Mahommed desist from his attempted innovations, and his insults to their gods,*
or to withdraw his protection from him. Abu Talib
thereupon discussed the question with his nephew
and tried his best to make him either to give up this
his enterprise, or at least make his efforts less vigorous
to achieve his object and to make his conduct less
offensive to his own people; but Mahommed had been
so much taken up with his hallucinations and the
grand scheme he had conceived, that he sturdily upheld
his convictions and designs, and said flatly that if these
people were to set up the sun against him on his right
and the moon on his left, he would still not give up the
accomplishment of his enterprise. Abu Talib was now
so much persuaded of his nephew's convictions that he
no more dared to argue with him on this subject, the
while he made the people to understand that his
nephew was really a messenger from God and therefore
they should take him as their spiritual leader and guide.
He promised his nephew in future always to stand by
his side against all his enemies and to defend him
against all their assaults. The hatred and frenzy of
the Koreish against him, on the contrary, increased

swearer, a despicable fellow, a defamer going about to slander,
. . . cruel, and besides this of spurious birth . . . we shall
stigmatize him on the nose' and tradition says this prophetical
menace was made good at the battle of Badr, where Walid had
his nose split. To reprove common swearing, condemn slander
and cruelty is legitimate enough, but to reproach any man with
his spurious birth betrays a degree of personal rancour altogether
unworthy of the prophetic character to which he pretended.
Yet the above are the words put into the mouth of the Almighty
and most Holy God ! ! !
    * The Koreish were deeply interested in the retention of that
idolatry, which made Mecca at once a centre of religious resort
and a flourishing and important commercial emporium. To
attack its idols was to attack Mecca's greatness itself.

and they began strenuously to oppose the teachings and
innovations of Mahommed; and when they found that
they could prevail neither by fair words or by violent
menaces to make him to desist from this his undertaking, they imagined that they could do so by force
and ill-treatment. They began to treat his followers
with great contempt and even to employ violence
against them and so harshly were they treated and so
violently were they continually attacked by these
infuriated people that it was no more possible or safe
for the followers of Mahommed to continue any longer
to remain in peace at Mecca. Once while Zeid the
slave and adopted son of the prophet was leading a
party of new converts in prayer, they were suddenly
attacked by the Meccans, but the Mahommedans boldly
defended themselves, and on this occasion Zeid struck
one of the assailants so violently with a camel's goad,
that it made the man bleed profusely, and thus the
first man's blood was spilt in the cause of Islam and
this blood, as we shall see in the following pages,
was to run in torrents while Islam was being propagated at the point of the sword by the prophet. Up
to this Mahommed used to hold his meetings and to
conduct the prayers in the house of Arkun, belonging
to one of his converts, close by the sanctuary of Kaaba,
but the continued insults and injuries heaped on him,
and the still grosser indignities and violent assaults
made on his followers so depressed the prophet of
Islam, that he deemed it prudent at last to buy peace by
seeking a compromise with the Meccans, by which he
approved the worship they paid to their most important
idols Lat, Uzz, and Manat and raised them to the
dignity of goddesses and intercessors (Koran, ch. 53).
The story runs thus ' One day he sat down among the
chief men of Mecca beside the Kaaba, and recited to
them the fifty-third sura including an account of the

first apparition of the angel to him, and also that of a later vision of the same heavenly spirit, when the following verse was revealed to him "What think ye of Al Lat and Al Uzz and Manat the third goddess with them?"' At this verse it is stated that the evil spirit suggested to Mahommed the words of compromise, 'These are the sublime females, whose intercession may be hoped for.' This concession on the part of the prophet of Allah, by which their gods Lat, Uzz, and Manat were acknowledged as true divine beings by the prophet, greatly pleased the people of Mecca, who up to this had been strenuously opposing him, and they began to treat Mahommed and his followers on friendly terms. But Mahommed soon repented of what he had done, attributing this concession or compromise to the weakness of his spirit and announced that in a subsequent apparition of the heavenly spirit, it had been revealed to him that Allah had erased that part of the Sura, in which the aforesaid compromise was written, making it now read after 'Manat third goddess' 'What?' . . . 'They are no other than empty names, which you and your fathers have invented.' The Meccans finding now that he had revoked the concession and broken the terms of the compromise, accused him of fraud, and renewed their hostilities with fresh vigour attacking him and his followers with redoubled violence, naming the prophet, not an apostle of Allah, but a seducer and a deceiver. Whereupon Mahommed finding it no longer possible for his followers to remain safe in Mecca gave permission to such of his converts as had no strong friends to protect them at Mecca, to seek refuge and shelter elsewhere. Accordingly in the fifth year of his mission, a party of his converts, sixteen in number, including Mahommed's daughter, Rakiah and her husband Othman, fled into Abyssinia. These refugees were not only kindly received by

Najashi the King of Ethiopia, but it is said he himself
after some time embraced Islam and became follower
of Mahommed; thus the seed of Islam went out of its
birth-place and began to sprout in a foreign soil, and
these sixteen fugitives became the first messengers of
Islam to a foreign people.

In the sixth year of his mission, amidst such dis-
couragements and afflictions, he had the good pleasure
of seeing his flock strengthened by the conversion of his
uncle Hamza, a man of great valour and merit; and also
of Omar, a person highly esteemed, and till lately
a violent opponent of the prophet—and of several other
important persons. Filled with great delight at these
conversions, the prophet exclaimed enthusiastically
'Allah Akbar,' God is great.

THE KOREISH LEAGUE — MAHOMMED AND HIS FOLLOWERS BOYCOTTED

As persecutions generally advance rather than obstruct
the spreading of a religion, Mahommedanism made in
the meantime so great a progress among the various
Arab tribes, that the Koreish alarmed at this success
of Mahommed, made a solemn league or covenant against
them with a view to harass and oppress his followers.
They bound themselves by a solemn engagement
not to contract any marriage with the followers of
Mahommed, nor to hold any kind of communication
with them, and further neither to sell to or to buy
anything from them and to give greater solemnity and
solidarity to the league, they reduced its terms to
writing and laid the document containing the terms in
the Kaaba. Upon this the tribe became divided into
two factions; and this state of things continued for
three years, during which time the followers of the
prophet, entirely isolated, had to suffer patiently all

these privations; supplies of food could be obtained
only with great difficulty, and that from foreign traders
and at exorbitant prices. At the close of the third year
of this convention which was the tenth of his mission,
Mahommed told his uncle Abu Talib that God had
shewn His disapproval of the league of the Koreish by
sending a worm to eat out every word of the document
placed in the Kaaba except the word Allah written on
the document. Mahommed very probably had some
private information of this incident, because during
these three years of ostracism, Mahommed mingled with
the pilgrims, and used to go often to Kaaba and there
to pass as much time as was possible for him under the
circumstances. Abu Talib assured of this occurrence
repaired to the chiefs of the Koreisites and told them
how God had disapproved of their league, and that His
disapproval had been revealed by God to His prophet as
well as the way how He had destroyed their document,
adding further that if what he had told them was found
true on the examination of the document, they should
lay aside all their animosities and ill-feelings towards
the followers of Mahommed; on the other hand, if it
should prove false, he would without any further
hesitation deliver up his nephew to their wishes.
They all most willingly agreed to these proposals and
went to inspect the document, and to their great
astonishment and confusion found everything narrated
by Abu Talib to be quite true, and thereupon the
league which was so long in force was declared null
and void.

THE DEATH OF KHADIJA AND ABU TALIB
MAHOMMED A POLYGAMIST

In the fiftieth year of his life, and the tenth of his
mission Mahommed lost his faithful wife Khadija, who

had been a very powerful support to further his designs and who had contributed so generously to his fortune. This loss was followed by the death of his uncle and guardian Abu Talib, which occurred only a few weeks after the death of his wife. As we have already seen Khadija not only helped Mahommed to be a very powerful man, but by the strength of her mind and mature experience had always maintained a decided ascendency over her husband, and had managed him with great wisdom and firmness. She was the first and foremost to give credit to her husband's heavenly inspirations and revelations as well as the first and foremost to accept the truth of his divine mission, and to proclaim him as the apostle and messenger of God; and therefore his sorrow and grief at her death was for some time very inconsolable, but the occupation of his mind in the furtherance of his enterprise soon made him forget this sorrow, though he retained the memory of her goodness and of her unwavering faith to the day of his death, and placed her name in the list of the four perfect women the world had seen. The Sura lxvii. gives the names of these four women who reached perfection, viz., Asia, the wife of Pharaoh; Mary, the mother of Jesus; Kadija, the wife of Mahommed; and Fatima, his daughter, the wife of Ali. To make up for the loss of his dear wife, within two months of her death he married Sauda, the widow of Sakram an early convert, and not content with one wife to supply the place of his dear lost wife, he at the same time bethrothed himself to Ayesha, then only seven years old, the younger daughter of his bosom friend Abu Bekr. Mahommed though he was now fifty years old, and thus had long ceased to be a young man, began at this time to give way to that gratification of lust and polygamy, which afterwards become a conspicuous and characteristic feature of his life.

FURTHER PERSECUTIONS

THE Koreish seeing that Mahommed was now deprived of his two best supporters, once again began to be more troublesome and mischievous than ever before to the prophet, so much so that it was necessary for him to seek refuge and shelter elsewhere. He therefore went first to Taif about sixty miles east of Mecca and commenced there to preach his doctrine, which however, was received very coldly by the people, who soon began to hate him, and he was so ill-treated by them, that he was obliged to fly from that place. This repulse greatly disheartened and discouraged his followers, but Mahommed though now sunk in the deepest despondency, tried to preserve the calmness of his mind, and maintaining an unshaken constancy did his best to keep up the spirits of his followers, and returning to Mecca made bold to preach his doctrine at all public places and especially to the great public assemblies at the pilgrimages. This brought to him a pretty good harvest and among the numerous conversions he had thus now made, he had the pleasure to find six people from Yathreb near Medina of the Jewish tribe of Khazraj. These people, when they returned home from the pilgrimage, spoke very highly of the new religion that was preached with such fervour by Mahommed, and which they had most willingly embraced and exhorted their fellow countrymen to follow their example by embracing the same.

MAHOMMED MEETS THE PEOPLE OF MEDINA

WHEN the time of pilgrimage came round again and people had assembled in great numbers at the place of the pilgrimage, Mahommed was there ready to preach his doctrine, and such was his fervour and earnestness in the preaching of his new doctrine, that a good many people, who had gathered there, began to listen attentively to his teachings.   Among this number of his earnest hearers, there was a small group of people who, drawn by curiosity at the report given by the six men of Yathreb, that had been to Mecca the previous year, had come from Medina, a place about 250 miles north of Mecca, and where as we have already seen, Abdullah the father of Mahommed had died, a short time before the birth of this his famous son and to which place also Mahommed had been taken by his mother Amina, when he was only six years old.   No doubt he interested himself very much in the people of this place and when he found that they shewed an unusual readiness to hear him and that they were all closely connected with the numerous Jews of that place, a new hope of finding a better field for his labour sprung into his heart, and he made several enquiries of them in order to ascertain if he and his followers would find a shelter and protection, as well as his doctrine many followers in their city. These people highly delighted at his teachings and greatly pleased at the interest he had taken in them, promised to make all the necessary enquiries and after sounding everyone carefully to give him all the information required when they returned in the following year to the pilgrimage.

In the meantime, on their return to their homes, they spoke to the people of Medina very enthusiastically of the doctrine they had heard preached to them with great fervour by the prophet at Mecca, and also spoke in very high terms of the prophet himself.

THE PLEDGE OF ACABA

THE Jews who were still expecting the Promised One or at least some great prophet to rise, when they heard

of Mahommed and of his doctrine, identified him with
their expected prophet, so much so a great many of
them expressed their desire to see Mahommed come to
their place and preach his doctrine to them.   When
the Jews of Medina came again on pilgrimage to Mecca
in the following year 621 A.D. and when they again
heard Mahommed preach to the people with the same
earnestness and fervour, such was their delight, that they
all went reverently in a body to the prophet to express
their profound respects to him, and further twelve men
of their number assured Mahommed of a very ripe
field for his mission work in their home and they bound
themselves by oath to Mahommed that they would
always remain faithful to him and they solemnly
promised to renounce idolatry and to obey the prophet
in all things that were reasonable ; this solemn oath,
which they took in a place called Acaba near Mecca is
known from that time as the pledge of Acaba (April,
621 A.D.).   Mahommed who had been very much disappointed at the ill-feelings of his own countrymen
towards him and his followers, was highly pleased at
this solemn promise made by the people of Medina and
form his part he promised them Paradise as a reward
for them, if they would remain faithful to their pledge ;
and immensely gratified at the bright prospects awaiting
for the great success of his doctrine at Medina, he sent
meantime one of his disciples by name Musab to preach
Islam to the people of Medina.   Musab by the assistance
of the twelve men soon after his arrival at Medina began
to preach in public the new religion of Mahommed, which
with the example of the twelve men, who had already
embraced it, had great effect on the people, many of
whom soon became converts to it.   Among these
proselytes of Medina, the most important was Osaid a
chief man of the city and Saad the prince of the
tribe of Aws. So rapidly did this doctrine spread in

that city, that there was scarcely a house wherein there was not some one of the followers of Islam.   Their idols were soon thrown aside, and many even of the hostile factions of the Aws and the Khajraj joined in the common devotions, and thus in a marvellous manner a purer theistic faith was substituted for the old superstitions of the Arab population.

MAHOMMED'S FICTION ; THE GREAT PRETENDED MIRACLE

MAHOMMED was pleased at the encouraging success his religion had met with, and the progress it had made everywhere, and full of hopes of a brilliant success in the near future for his enterprise by which he would be raised above all men ; in the meantime in the twelfth year of his mission to establish firmly his authoriity among his followers, he devised a strange plan.   When many of his followers had gathered for the customary prayers, he solemnly announced to them this his dream of a Night-Journey (Lailat-al-miraj) from Mecca to heaven by way of Medina and Jerusalem, a real fiction of his vivid imagination, that the Allah was pleased to favour him with a grand vision, in which he was carried by the angel Gabriel on a white-winged horse called Buraq from Mecca through Medina to the temple of Jerusalem and thence to heaven, and there he was made to stand in the presence of Allah, and there conversed with God and there received from Him many new precepts and commands to His people.   When his followers heard him relate this ridiculous story, vouched by no testimony whatever, it seemed to them so absurd and incredible, that several of them were staggered and were about to abandon him and his religion for good and probably his whole design and enterprise would have been thus totally ruined, had not Abu Bekr stepped forward in time and solemnly vouched for its veracity

C

and persuaded the people to accept it as a perfectly true thing. Upon the rock on which the mosque of Omar stands in Jerusalem, there is still shown what is called the print of Mahommed's foot, which he had left behind as he leaped therefrom upon the winged horse Buraq. This fabrication of a vision was one of the most artful contrivances Mahommed ever attempted to put into trial and it owed its success to the intervention of his bosom friend Abu Bekr, who was always quite ready to swallow blindly any kind of pill Mahommed would administer, and this success increased the prophet's credit and reputation to such a degree, that he was now sure of being able to make his disciples accept whatever he was pleased to impose upon them and it greatly contributed to the raising of his general credit and good name to that great height to which it afterwards arrived.

THE CONVERTS OF MEDINA AND THE SECOND PLEDGE OF ACCABA

THE next year Musab returned from Medina to Mecca accompanied by a band of seventy-three men and two women, of those who had embraced the Islam. On their arrival, they immediately went to Mahommed and having paid their profound reverence and respects to him, they offered him their assistance of which he was now in very great need, for his enemies were by this time grown so powerful in Mecca, that it was not possible for him to stay much longer there, without great danger to his life. The Koreish seeing that all their attempts to check the progress of the innovations introduced by their uncontrollable countryman had quite failed and that they could not in any way restrain the influence he and his followers were gaining everywhere, began to contemplate open violence to the prophet and his disciples, nay they even contemplated his murder should they still fail in their fresh attempts to curb him. Mahommed therefore in March 622 convened a general meeting of all his followers to concert measures for the safety of his own life as well as the lives of his followers, whereupon seventy persons of those who had come from Medina stood up and again solemnly pledged themselves to defend the prophet against all insults and assaults at the risk of their lives and took a solemn oath to that effect in March 622; and this oath is called the second pledge of Accaba, from the place where the meeting was held and where they again took this oath. Mahommed was highly pleased at this forwardness and generosity of his converts of Medina and in recompense he promised paradise to all those who might be killed in the defence of the prophet and intimated to them his intention of going with them to Medina. He next chose twelve persons out of their number, saying, that as Moses had chosen twelve leaders from amongst his people and as Jesus elected twelve apostles, in like manner, he too would have twelve out of their number to be sureties for the rest and they were to have the same authority among his followers as the twelve apostles of Jesus had among His disciples.

KOREISH FRESH PERSECUTIONS—MAHOMMED FLIES TO MEDINA—'HEJIRA'

THE Koreish having discovered the true object of the general meeting of his followers convened by Mahommed and the true nature of the famous convention he had entered into with the people of Medina at the place called Accaba, renewed their hatred and persecutions with greater determination and with redoubled ferocity. The prophet on the other hand, having now made sufficient provision for the safety both of his followers and of himself by the solemn treaty and pledge of Accaba, gave permission to his followers to repair to Medina, since it had pleased the Allah to give them a new brotherhood and a secure refuge in that city. Thus in April of the year 622 A.D. the first flight called by Mussulmans Hejira began, and hence from this incident and from this date the Moslem chronology begins. The emigration went on quietly and stealthily for the most part, house after house occupied by the followers of the prophet at Mecca being found abandoned. Within two months about 150 people succeeded in reaching Medina and at last only Mahommed, Abu Bekr and Ali were left behind at Mecca, because Mahommed alleged that he had not up to then received the sanction from heaven to quit his birthplace Mecca. Meanwhile the Koreish dreading the evil consequences of the new alliance with the people of Medina and beholding with alarm the exodus of the followers of the prophet, kept a very strict watch over the movements of Mahommed and immediately entered into a strong conspiracy to prevent the escape of Mahommed to Medina under any circumstances, and meantime took measures to secure his person and to put him to death. This secret conspiracy was scarce formed when by some means or other it came to Mahommed's knowledge.

The prophet, alarmed and frightened at this diabolical plot of his enemies, lost no time in announcing to the few chosen followers who had remained behind with him that he had received at last the permission from Allah communicated to him through the Angel Gabriel that he could now without any further delay, repair to Medina and there spend his zeal and energy to advance and propagate the religion that had been revealed to him. Whereupon under cover of night he

left his house without being observed by anyone
taking Abu Bekr alone with him, and took shelter in
the cave of Mount Thur some six miles distant from
Mecca, and there they hid themselves for three days
to escape the search of his enemies, which however
was very nearly successful. Here food was conveyed
to them stealthily during night by Abdullah and
Asma the children of Abu Bekr, and they had a
plentiful supply of milk brought them by a faithful
shepherd. The Koreish, exasperated at the sudden
and clandestine escape of Mahommed, immediately
arranged search parties and did their best to trace his
whereabouts. Abu Bekr, who had been secretly
informed of all the movements of the Koreisites,
finding that the prophet was now in imminent danger of
being discovered, imprisoned and murdered, grew
very sad, and was much disquieted. Mahommed,
who up to this had not fully realised the very risky
and precarious position in which he was, noticing his
bosom friend so troubled and careworn, encouraged
and comforted him with these really sublime words,
'We are two here, but God in the midst a third.'
There is perhaps no incident in the life of the prophet
which more nearly touches the sublime, which sets his
courage, his calm unwavering trust in God, in a more
exalted light than the life of three days he passed in this
cave of Mount Thur, a quite barren mountain, where the
assassination of the prophet and of his bosom-friend
might have been perpetrated unseen by a mortal eye,
had they been only discovered by his murderers. At the
close of the third day Ali, who had been left behind to
settle some business at Mecca and to make arrangments
for the safety of the families of Mahommed and of Abu
Bekr who had been left behind at Mecca, where they
were to remain for some time longer, with very great
precaution joined them under cover of the night. The

safe return of Ali greatly improved the spirits both of
Mahommed and Abu Bekr, and on the evening of the
fourth day, 20th June, they set out on their journey to
Medina, where they arrived on the 28th June 622 A.D.
and thus in the thirteenth year of his mission and in
the 53rd year of his age the Hejira or flight from Mecca
to Medina was completed towards the close of June
622 A.D., and within a few weeks the members of the
families of Mahommed and Abu Bekr who had remained
behind at Mecca, set out leisurely and without
molestation, and joined the rest of the fugitives at
Medina.

MAHOMMED AND THE SWORD

HITHERTO Mahommed had propagated his religion by
fair means, so that the whole success of his enterprise
amidst such persecutions and adversities, before his
flight to Medina, must be attributed to persuasion only
and not to any compulsion.   We have already seen how
the state of affairs both political and religious in Arabia
at the time of the birth of Mahommed had greatly
prepared the way for Mahommed's extraordinary success,
and it is no wonder, therefore, if the religion of
Mahommed which after all was much superior to the
gross idolatry practised in general by the people
of Arabia, appealed to the minds of many of the
Arabs, and made such progress among them notwithstanding the many persecutious and adversities it had to
meet with.   In several places of the Koran which were
revealed, as he alleged, during his stay at Mecca, he
declares in plain words that his business was only to
preach and admonish the people and that he had no
authority whatever to compel any person to embrace the
religion against his will and further whether the people

believed in him and in his doctrine or not, was none of
his concern, but belonged solely unto God.   And he was
so far from allowing his followers to use any force, that
he even exhorted them to bear patiently all injuries
which were offered them on account of their faith, nay
even he by divine authority permitted his followers,
under certain circumstances, to deny their faith, so long
as their heart was steadfast in it (sura xvi. 108) a
permission undoubtedly subversive of all morality ; and
when he himself was persecuted he chose rather to quit
the place of his birth and to retire to some foreign place,
than to make any resistance.   But this marked passive-
ness and moderation were due entirely to his want
of power and to the great superiority of his opponents
for the first twelve years of his mission ; for no sooner
was he enabled by the assistance of the converts in
Medina to make headway against his enemies, than he
gave out that God had allowed him and his followers to
defend themselves against infidels and at last as his
power and forces increased, he pretended to have received
the divine precept even to attack the infidels and destroying their idolatry to set up the true faith by the sword,
for he considered that his design and enterprise would
otherwise make but slow progress.

   That Mahommed had a right to take up arms for his
own defence against his unjust persecutors, may perhaps
be allowed, but whether he ought afterwards to have
made use of the sword for the advancement of his
religion, is a question not fit to be discussed here.   The
method of converting by the sword gives no very favourable opinion of the faith which is so propagated.   It is
certainly one of the most convincing proofs that Islamism
was no other than a pure human invention and owed
its progress and establishment almost entirely to the
sword, as we shall see in the following pages ; whereas
it is one of the strongest demonstrations in favour of

the superhuman origin of Christianity that it prevailed against all the forces and powers of the world by the mere force of its own truth, after having stood the assaults of all manner of persecutions and opposition for three hundred consecutive years.

PART SECOND

MAHOMMED AT MEDINA

YATHEIL, or as it is commonly called Medina, was a very rich and fertile city, enjoying every blessing of nature that an Eastern mind could desire and was likewise a prosperous commercial place. It was inhabited by the powerful Arab tribes, the Aws and the Khazrites. Jews formed a minority of its population during the time of Mahommed; they had settled themselves in this place, after their sacred city Jerusalem had been taken by the Romans, and they themselves dispersed. Though they formed a small community still they were far superior to the Arabs in culture, and were better equipped with instruments for agriculture, and understood many industries to which the Arabs were total strangers. Thus the Jews of Medina, by the aid of their peaceful industry, had acquired considerable wealth and at the time of Mahommed, though they formed comparatively a small part of the population, still they were very rich and powerful. The Arabs, however, formed the bulk of the population of the city.

It was to this beautiful and fertile town of Medina, which already included a number of adherents of Mahommed, that Mahommed with his companions was

now repairing with sanguiue hopes, for he had been
made to believe that this place was far more favourable
for the execution of his designs than Mecca.

The news of the arrival of the great prophet of Islam
soon spread everywhere, and many of his converts
prepared themselves to accord a befitting welcome to
the great prophet.

The fatigue of the long journey of about 375 miles,
as well as other anxieties, induced Mahommed to rest
awhile on his way before he entered the city. He
therefore made a halt at Kuba a suburb of Medina, now
famous for its gardens and orchards. Here his neophytes did their best to offer every possible hospitality
to the prophet and his companions. The news of his
arrival and stay at Kuba as well as of the day of his
solemn entry into the city were soon communicated to
his converts at Medina. Though Kuba was so close to
Medina, the fact was none of its inhabitants came to
see him at Kuba, though he stayed at this place for
about fourteen days, made Mahommed very suspicious
and cautious and he spent the time finding out the
truth about the welcome he was to receive in the new
city. After he had received the desired information,
on the appointed day (a Friday,) Mahommed left
Kuba, seated on a camel with Abu Bekr behind
him. At a place called Wadi Raunah midway between
Kuba and Medina, he halted again and performed his
first Friday service, giving a sermon on the new faith
to the neophytes who had followed him. From that
day to this, in commemoration of this solemn day,
Friday has been the Mahommedan Sunday. The
journey from this place was a grand triumphal procession, for his converts had spared nothing to accord
a most hearty and joyous welcome to their great prophet.
Mahommed was well pleased with the hearty welcome
given to him by his converts, and he gave them a short

sermon bidding them show their joy by goodwill
to their neighbours, by mutual charity, by increased
family unity and by prayer, promising them that thus
they should enter Paradise in peace.

It is asserted that each tribe by which he passed
desired the honour of his presence and requested him
to take up his abode with them ; that he refused all
these offers, in order to excite no jealousy and left it to
the camel on which he rode to decide the question.
The camel entered the eastern quarter and lay down in
a large open courtyard near Abu Ayoub's house ; in
that house therefore Mahommed took up his temporary
residence for about seven months, that is, until a house
of prayer with proper residences for his wives had been
built in the court yard. Here his table was amply
supplied by the voluntary offerings of the Faithful.
This court yard or piece of ground which had
before served to put camels in and belonged to the
orphan sons of Amru, was taken by unfair means from
its owners (as Dr Prideux in his Life of Mahommed says),
and thus the first fabric or mosque of Islam worship
was built on a site, which was acquired by the same
doubtful means as those by which the prophet propagated his religion. However, other historians say
that the place was bought by Abu Bekr for the prophet.

THE FIRST MOSQUE OF ISLAM

THE first year of Mahommed's residence at Medina
was chiefly occupied in building the great mosque
about 100 cubits (150 feet) square, which was roofed
with palm tree trunks covered in with palm wood
rafters ; on one side of the mosque he constructed
apartments for himself and his wives, and on the
other side rooms for poor adherents who had no
houses of their own.

Some historians, however, say that Mahommed in the
very beginning did not go to the trouble of building
a new mosque but utilised a barn or storehouse which
was close to the court-yard, and which was purchased
for a small sum. The barn had a roof of palm branches
and clay, not sufficiently solid to keep out rain. It is
probable that Mahommed spent the time in enlarging
the barn and in making such repairs and alterations as
would make it serve for a mosque as well as quarters for
himself, and constructed also suitable dwellings for
his wives around it, the most famous being the one
which he built for his wife Ayesha, then in her tenth
year, and which, for the consummation of her nuptials,
she took possession of with unostentatious pomp, and
which was in years after destined to be the burial
place of her husband the great prophet of Islam.
Though this mosque was comparatively very small
and built with rude materials, yet it is glorious in
the history of Islam as having been the first mosque
of Mahommed. Here the prophet and his companions
spent the greater part of their time; here the daily
exercises were first publicly established, here the great
congregation assembled every week and heard the
sermons of the prophet; here he planned his victories
and here from this spot he sent forth envoys to kings
and emperors, with the summons to embrace Islam; it
was here that each fresh revelation was delivered to
him, and in fine it was here that the great Prophet of
Islam yielded up the ghost and here he lies buried.

To Mahommed the world consisted of only two classes of men, namely, those who acknowledged his mission and thereby became believers and those who rejected it, and who were called hypocrites¹ meaning 'those in whose hearts is sickness.' The Jews were not unaware of the notion of what a prophet should be like, and we have already seen they formed a powerful and rich community in Medina, and therefore Mahommed wished to conciliate the Jews as far as possible. He did not also forget that the sources of information about prophets, revelation, angels, etc. to both Meccans and Medinese were Jews, and Mahommed greatly relied on Jewish witnesses. He even adopted many of their opinions, doctrines and customs, thereby to draw them to his side. The Jews on the other hand would not accept him as their prophet because he did not come from Syria as they always expected the prophets to rise from Syria alone; nor as their law-giver in the place of or even in addition to Moses, one who was quite ignorant of their Hebrew language; much less as the greater prophet spoken of in the Jewish Scriptures which Mahommed claimed himself to be, because he was not born of the seed of David or of any Jewish blood. The Jews, therefore, who would not acknowledge his pretended claims, began to grow envious of him because Mahommed was growing in power by the use of their scriptures, of which he had very small knowledge and therefore they tried to discredit him before his followers. A certain Jew even took the trouble to translate a portion of the Old Testament into Arabic, in the hope of ruining the prophet's reputation. But Mahommed refused to grant permission to his followers to read the book,

saying, 'If Moses himself were to come to life, you
would have no right to follow him and abandon me.'
Disputes, leading to violence, broke out between the
Jews and Mahommed's fanatical followers, which soon
produced mutual contempt and dislike.   The Jews
too professed disgust at a prophet whose chief concern
was his harem.   Mahommed now saw that the Jews
were plotting to ruin him or at least seriously to harm
him, and being now securely settled at Medina and
able not only to defend himself against the insults
of his enemies, but even to attack them, his attitude
towards the Jews began to gradually change.   In
his earlier inspirations he had spoken of them as
the chosen of heaven, and their books as having
divine authority, but now intensely irritated at their
obstinate conduct, he began to attack them, pronouncing
them to be idolatrous, accusing them of rejecting their
Messiah, and of systematically concealing all the
passages in their scriptures foretelling his advent.
Till now he had considered Jerusalem as the chief
sacred place 'Kibla'; and had ruled that all should
turn towards that sacred place during prayer; but
now pretending a revelation, he ordered his followers
to turn themselves towards the Kaaba at Mecca.   He
also confirmed his intention of making Friday the
Mahommedan Sacred day, because the Jews held the
Saturday as their Sabbath.   In fine he conceived the
idea of eventually extirpating and destroying the Jews
because   he   secretly   recognised   their   superior
knowledge of matters of which he claimed authority.
The knowledge of scriptures which the Jews had
was very dangerous to him, and their learning was
sufficient to irritate him, and thus they were more
than a match for a man who had very little learning
and who did not even know that the year was
determined by the relations between the earth and

the sun. The feeling began soon to be embittered,
and the Jews of Medina soon began to feel the power
and hostility of the Prophet's arm.

MAHOMMED THE LAW-GIVER

To please the Jews Mahommed had adopted the Jewish
Day of Atonement as a Mahommedan fast day also and
now he established his own peculiar fasts, called the
great fast during the sacred month of Ramadan, ordain-
ing a total abstinence from food, drink and all enjoyments on fast days from sunrise till sunset, but everything
was allowed after sunset till next sunrise. He also ruled
that the month of the fast should be closed by a festival
called 'the breaking of the fast,' during which abundant
alms should be given to the poor. He moreover
established a day of Sacrifice on which day two fat kids
were sacrificed by the prophet. The direction of
position during prayer having been changed as we have
already observed, he now ordered the performance of
Satat or prayers five times in a day namely *at dawn, at
noon, midtime between noon and sunset; just after sunset* and *midtime between sunset and midnight.* He
moreover, considered the use of bells as unbecoming
and improper, and established a spiritual call for prayer
ascribing its sanction to a divine revelation. He made
his negro servant Belal ascend a lofty wall near the
mosque early before daybreak and proclaim in a loud
voice, 'Great is Alhah, I bear witness that there is
no God but Alhah, I bear witness that Mahommed is the
Prophet of Alhah, come to prayers, come unto happiness,
Great is Alhah' and it was ruled that the same call for
prayer should be repeated at the commencement of each
of the five times of the Satat or prayer. Mahommed to
increase his dignity during discourses, constructed a
pulpit, the platform of which was raised three steps

above the floor and placed it near the southern side wall
of the mosque. It became an object of great sanctity to
Mahommedans. From this pulpit Mahommed turning
towards Kaaba would conduct the services, deliver
discourses on Fridays, and after performing the prescribed prostrations and prayers, would recite portions
of the Koran. As he discoursed he leant upon a staff.
His dress on these occasions was a mantle of striped
stuff, six cubits in length, thrown over his shoulders;
the lower garment was a girdle of fine cloth, but of
smaller dimensions than the other. These robes were
worn only on Fridays and on the two great festivals;
at the conclusion of each service they were folded up
and put carefully away. Mahommed's close touch with
Jews and Christians had taught him to assign a far
higher importance to the subject of clean and unclean
food; he therefore forebade his followers the use of
blood, meats offered to idols, strangled beasts and
swine flesh, which all were considered to be unclean
and unlawful.

MAHOMMED A BELLIGERENT

THE latter life of Mahommed may be considered as a
period of war and politics even more than of religion,
or rather his religion became identified with war and
politics. From the time of his flight to Medina, though
the Meccans abstained from active hostilities, he had
threatened divine vengeance against them and was
only waiting for a suitable time. When he saw himself
securely settled at Medina and able to attack his enemies
he began to send out small parties to make reprisals on
the Koreish. He knew that the Meccans, who had
driven him and his followers away from their ances-
tral homes, were merchants, and their caravans, laden
with wealth of all kinds, were constantly passing

between Arabia and Syria by the route near Medina. Surely to despoil these infidels and employ their property to feed the hungry and to clothe the naked among the people of God, the greater part of whom had been driven away from their fatherland and were now reduced to great want and distress, would be a work well pleasing in the sight of God. Mahommed was not long in obtaining a revelation sanctioning this highway robbery. Parties were accordingly organised and dispatched in different directions to intercept the Meccan caravans. The first party that Mahommed had sent out to make reprisals on the Koreish consisted of no more than nine under the command of fanatic Abdullah, a cousin of Mahommed, who intercepted and plundered a caravan belonging to the Koreish at Nakhlah, in November 623, which was travelling unarmed and without escort under cover of the sacred month, during which time it was unlawful to fight or to shed blood, and in this action one of the Koreish, a Hadramite, was killed by one Wakid under the command of Abdullah, and two were taken prisoners. They then returned to Medina with the whole booty. This was the first booty the Muslims captured, the seed of those to follow hereafter, the first prisoner they seized, and the first life they took ; and this all happened in the sacred month held inviolable even by the Pagan Arabs. We cannot detail here the marauding expeditions that were sent out by Mahommed from this time afterwards with varying success. Some Arabs at Medina were displeased that Mahommed allowed war and plunder during the sacred months, but Mahommed declared that he was justified by a revelation which told him that though war during sacred months was grievous, yet infidelity towards God, keeping men from the holy temple and driving out God's people from thence was still more grievous.

D

THE INCENTIVES TO WAR

THE warlike spirit, so temptingly combining religious incentives with those of plunder, grew apace, and Mahommed produced a revelation in favour of war against unbelievers until all opposition ceased and there was no religion but Alhah's; 'kill them,' he said 'wheresoever you find them, expel them from that out of which they have expelled you; fight not however in the Holy Temple unless they fight with you in that place,' and he promised Paradise in return to those who fell in battle.   Contributions were solicited towards war, and a higher place was to be granted to those who contributed before the victory; 'who is he that lendeth unto the Lord a good loan?   He shall double the same and he shall have an honourable recompense.'   He thus maintained his armed forces partly by the contributions of his followers for this purpose, which he called by the name of *zacat* or alms, and the paying of which he very artfully made a main article of his faith, with a bright promise of a higher place in Paradise for those who paid this zacat generously; and partly they were maintained by ordering that a fifth part of all plunder and booty should be brought into the public treasury to be spent by the Prophet according to his good pleasure.

THE BATTLE OF BADR

THE death of the Hadramite, who was killed by Wakid under the command of Abdullah at Nakhlah in the foremost of the reprisals, had important results. This man and his brother were under the protection of Utbah, a Koreisite of great power and influence; the protector in such a case was bound to avenge the death of his client.   Between the people of Mecca and the prophet there was now a blood-feud.

A caravan under the command of the famous Abu
Sufyan, and laden with goods of the value of over five
hundred thousand francs was returning from Syria.
The prize was worthy of an effort and Mahommed, who
had his spies every where to furnish him with all such
information, no sooner was apprised of it, than he at
once called his followers to arms ; every one wished to
share in the plunder, and about 300 of the strongest of
his followers rallied around him ; Abu Sufyan, however,
having received timely information of the raid, hurried
to Mecca by unsuspected routes and by forced marches,
and also sent a scout to call the Meccans to help. Hearing this message the Meccans, who were thirsting for
vengeance, resolved on a general rally, in which all
men took part. Having discovered Mahommed's plan
to intercept the route where it passed near Medina,
the Meccans about 1000 strong hastened thither. Both
armies met in January, 624, at a place called Badr.
Mahommed before the fighting began drew up his
troops in line of battle, which struck Utbah the Meccan
general with amazement. Soon a bloody battle ensued.
The Meccan Arabs unacquainted with military science
and discipline, fought without any order or arrange-
ment. Mahommed on the contrary did his best to
maintain order and to keep up the spirits of his fighting
men. Discipline and steadfastness of purpose are said
to win battles, and these qualities were conspicuous
on the Moslem side and not on the Meccan, and thus
the Meccans though far superior in number, were deci-
sively routed, fifty of their number being slain, among
whom were their general Utbah and his colleague
Abu-Jahl the leader of the Meccans and a great
enemy of the prophet ; and a great many were made
prisoners and the rest took to flight. Thus was
started that career of bloodshed and conquest, which
has distinguished Mahommadanism more than any

other religion. Mahommed regarded this victory as
a miracle and ascribed it to the intervention of the
Angels Gabriel and Michael, who with 3000 angels
flew as whirlwinds at the enemy and put them to
flight. It is no great wonder that 300 well disciplined
and fanatic men aided by 3000 angels should defeat
1000 undisciplined men when there have been instances
in which a small band of men have utterly defeated
tenfold their number, without the help of the angels!
No event in the history of Islam was of more importance
than this battle of Badr and the Koran rightly calls it
' the day of Deliverance,' the day before which Moslems
were weak, and after which they became strong and
formidable. This battle is also memorable, because on
this occasion Mahommed for the first time drew his
sword in assertion of his claim as the commissioned
Apostle of the Most High God, and the victory was
alleged to be a sign of its truth, and Mahommed was
received in triumph on his return to Medina. After the
battle the three days he remained at Badr were spent
in butchering the prisoners ; first of all two prisoners
whom Mahommed hated personally were put to death,
then a woman by name Asma who had steadfastly clung
to the faith of her fathers, and who had composed some
verses against Mahommed and his religion was put to
death in cold blood while she was asleep with her
babe by her side ; and then those who either did not
embrace the new faith or did not free themselves by
payment of heavy ransoms were cruelly put to death.
The rich spoils of Badr were distributed among his
followers one fifth being reserved for God and his
prophet. Wealth, fame, honour, and power were now
secured to Mahommed on this grand day of deliverance,
and in consideration of this victory he was ready to the
end of his life to forgive any offence committed by any
one who had taken part in this fight.

The new religion shewed that it was to be founded upon human passions, upon pride of domination, upon fanaticism, quite as much as upon simplification of truth and belief about God. The very process of winning the first victory became in the hands of Mahommed and his principal followers, a method of strengthening their convictions and at the same time their hold upon their followers. After this battle the people of Medina renewed their pledge and swore to follow Mahommed whithersoever he went or desired them to fight.

MAHOMMED AND THE JEWS AGAIN

BLOODSHED leads to bloodshed. Mahommed could now brook no opposition. We have already seen how Mahommed had at last made up his mind to destroy the Jews, whom he considered as his greatest enemies. The Jews, whose ill-luck rarely failed them, signalised themselves by offensive sneers and poor epigrams against the prophet whenever an occasion offered them to do so. Whenever Mahommed experienced reverses during his earlier raids, the sneers from the Jews became louder and their sarcasms more stinging. Mahommed lost patience with them after long endurance of their jibes; and a more serious step had to be taken against those Jews under the leadership of Beni Kainuka who inhabited the chief market of Medina. They were goldsmiths and doubtless the wealthiest of the inhabitants of Medina. About a month after the prophet's return from Badr a dispute broke out between him and the Beni Kainuka, which led to the denunciation of the treaty he had made with the people of Medina on his first entry into their city, and he attacked the dwellings of the Jewish goldsmiths against the terms of the treaty. The other Jewish tribes remained quite indifferent at the crisis that had befallen

their brethren, a proof how grievous were the internal
dissensions and mutual animosities that were prevalent
among the Jews of Medina about this time. Many of
the Jews were massacred by the prophet's order and
the rest were ordered to vacate their dwellings. Their
possessions were treated by the prophet as the spoils
of war. He took his fifth share and divided the rest
among his followers. The banishment of the Beni-
Kainuka apparently led the other Jewish tribes to
reflect on the fate that was in store for them, but it did
not move them to any coalition or combined action.
Meanwhile, Mahommed ordered the assassination of a
wealthy and influential Jew by name Kab-ibn-Ashraff
of the Nadirite tribe, because he was considered to be
intriguing with the Meccans against the prophet.
The supposed conspiracy of Kab further gave Mahommed an adequate ground for outlawing all the Jews
then inhabiting Medina. Thus tribe after tribe of
Jews were either compelled to submit to the faith
of Islam or were expelled and exterminated. For a
whole year after the battle of Badr the prophet's
power kept on increasing and fortune continued favourable. Partly by conquest and partly by treaty the
country which lay between Medina and Mecca towards
the coast was soon won to the prophet's side.

About this time another heavily laden caravan started
from Mecca by a quite new route, but Mahommed soon
became informed of it and sent his adopted son Laid
with an expedition to capture the convoy, which he
did very successfully, and came near capturing Abu
Sufyan himself. The property seized on this occasion
is said to have been of the value of 100,000 dirkems.

MAHOMMED A DEBAUCHEE

SENSUALITY followed hard on bloodshed. The accession
of wealth now enabled the prophet to add to his harem,
which now began to assume princely dimensions. New
wives were constantly added to his harem, and from
this time (624) there was scarcely a year of his life in
which he did not take a new wife. He gave his daughter
Fatima, then seventeen years old, in marriage to Ali
twenty-five years old; he likewise gave to his friend
Othman his daughter Umm Kulthum, as a substitute
for Rokaya who had died during the battle of Badr.

Mahommed's taste and delight being generally known
as well as the object of his secret amusements, the
tribes that were anxious to gain his favour, presented
him with the fairest of their women. We have
already seen that soon after the death of Khadija his
first wife, he had married Sauda and had betrothed
himself to Ayesha the younger daughter of his friend
Abu Bekr, and the marriage with Ayesha was celebrated
soon after his arrival at Medina. After a short time he
added yet another wife to his harem and two years
afterwards he added another. Mahommed happening
one day to visit the house of his adopted son Zaid on
some affair and not finding him at home, accidentally
cast his eyes on Zeinab the wife of Zaid, who was then
in a dress which discovered her beauty to advantage,
and being smitten at the sight of the beautiful woman,
and bewildered by the charms of her beauty, uttered a
cry of passionate admiration, 'God be praised, who
turneth the hearts of men as he pleaseth.' These words
were overheard by Zainab, who, proud of her conquest,
told her husband of it on his return home. Whereupon
Zaid, after mature reflection, thought he could do no
other than part with his wife in favour of his benefactor
and therefore resolved to divorce her and acquainted

Mahommed with his resolution.   Mahommed apprehend-
ing the scandal it might cause, for a time deferred
his marriage with the wife of his adopted son, because
the old Arabs considered that the relationship by
adoption created the same impediment of marriage as
if it had been real blood relationship, and therefore
the prophet's marrying Zainab the wife of his adopted son
Zaid would cause great scandal.   However, being unable to stifle the flames of love for Zainab that inwardly
consumed him, he pretended to have received a revelation
from God by which he was authorised to take Zainab
for his wife, and accordingly after the term of her
divorce was expired, he married her in the latter end of
the fifth year of Hejira, June 626, and when his
followers began to murmur about this scandalous
marriage, he quoted to them the 33 sura of the Koran
containing the following passage : '*And when Zaid had
fulfilled her divorce, we joined thee with her in marriage,
that there might hereafter be no offence to believers in
marrying the wives of their adopted sons after that they
have divorced them.*'   He likewise declared that the
existing custom of the impediment was unreasonable
and abolished it for the future ; moreover he disallowed
the custom of adoption for the future among his
followers (sura 33).   Though he had fixed the legal
number of four wives at a time for his followers, he
gave out that God had allowed him as a special
privilege to have any number of wives and even to
cohabit with his female slaves taken as captives, if he
liked to do so.   The same sura 33 runs thus : '*O
prophet, we allowed thee thy wives, whom thou hast
dowered and also the slaves whom thy right hand
possesseth of the booty . . . and any believing woman, who
hast given herself up to the prophet; in case the prophet
desireth to take her to wife.   This is a peculiar privilage
granted unto thee above the rest of the true believers.*'

It is impossible to avoid wondering at the strange
credulity of his followers, who, with seemingly un-
diminished faith, allowed him the aid of inspiration as
a pander to his personal predilections. This conduct
of Mahommed, who thus pretended to have married the
fair Zainab by the will and sanction of heaven under a
special revelation from God, is considered by all writers
as an act of most impious effrontery, and the pretended
relaxation of the marriage rules in his own favour as the
greatest and indelible stain on his memory. It is also
strange to see that he now laid down rules under special
revelation from heaven (sura xxxiii.) regarding the
conduct to be observed by visitors. Guests and strangers
are not to enter his habitations uninvited ; they are to
use no familiarity and they are to speak to his wives
only from behind a curtain and thus they are to give no
uneasiness to the apostle of God in this respect and
above all his followers are strictly forbidden to marry
his wives at any time, even after his own death. One
can reflect here how the prophet of God maliciously
suspected the like mean and treacherous conduct in
others, that was so conspicuous in his own life.

Moreover it may be well in this place to consider what
the teaching of the Koran is on the subject of the
plurality of wives. In sura iv. permission is given to
the Faithful to take two or three or four and not more,
women as wives and in addition to these they can have as
concubines any number of slave girls which their right
hand possesses, that is purchased or made captives in
war. In fact though the number of wives permitted
for a follower of Mahommed is restricted to four, practically this number is unlimited because the Koran in the
same sura allows an almost unchecked power of divorce
and exchange. The power of the husband, who is ex-
pressly stated to be far superior to the wife, is almost
uncontrolled. He may repudiate his wives without any

assigned reason and even without warning ; she is more
to be as a kind of play thing, existing simply to satisfy
the lust of man and for labour and who could be
capriciously flung aside at one's pleasure ; her condition
as wife is worse than that of a slave. The same sura
even allows the husband to rebuke, strike and even
imprison his wife if she be found disobedient and the
poor wife has almost no means of redress, except that
she can claim the balance of her dowry, generally a very
insignificant sum, and maintenance for three months.
Such a system is intolerable to a feeling heart and
consistent only with the social degradation of the female
sex. The majority of Mahommedans, however at present,
constrained by poverty or custom, content themselves
with one wife and though such marriages may be and
doubtless are often happy ones, still the wife, under the
licence of the Koran, has continually hanging over her
head the apprehension of divorce and this cannot but
prove an abiding source of uneasiness to her. However
exemplary and devoted her conduct, she may at any
moment be called upon to quit her home and her
children and see her place occupied by some younger
and more favoured stranger. Some Mahommedans
make a habit of continually changing their wives. It
is not an uncommon thing to find young men who have
had twenty or thirty wives, a new one every three or
four months ; and thus it happens that women are liable
to be transferred indefinitely from one man to another,
and are obliged to accept a husband and a home wherever they can find one ; or in case of destitution, to which
divorce may have reduced them, resort to other more
degrading means of living. Mahommed in giving
permission to his followers to have more wives than
one and in even himself thus giving practical effect to
this his sanction of polygamy, might to some extent be
excused and he may not be held personally blameable

for the step he thus took. Polygamy was universally practised about this time all over the East; many Arabs had eight to ten wives. It is rather to the credit of Mahommed that he restrained this polygamy within narrower bounds. Moreover in the histories of the Old Testament, of which he had been no idle student, he would find numerous examples of its practice by patriarchs and kings with the tacit approval or at least without any expressed reproval from a higher power; and though this practice has been condemned by the purer teaching of Christianity, we cannot assume that he was aware of this fact. However, though he may have been alive to the evil effects of polygamy then generally practised in Arabia both by Arabs and Jews without any restraint, it was what his own sensual appetite and lust craved and what was considered a privilege for his pleasure-seeking followers, and it may be well supposed that he shrank from the task of setting himself to work against the practice, the most cherished both for himself and for his followers. It may therefore be concluded that either the practical working of this abominable practice failed to impress on the mind of the prophet, deluded with his own sensuality, the desirability of interfering with the existing custom, or that, blinded by his passions, he wilfully neglected to contemptate seriously the practical evil results of his legislation. In sanctioning the practice of polygamy in the Koran as a divine revelation, he must undoubtedly be held responsible for the long train of degrading consequences, which have followed the licence thus established.

Further it may be noted here that so long as this unlimited permission of cohabitation with their female slaves continues it cannot be hoped that there will be a very hearty attempt to put a stop to slavery, whatever form it takes, in Mahommedan countries. Though Mahommed

in some respects, undoubtedly ameliorated the condition
of slaves, still he looked upon slavery as a permanent
institution (sura xxiv.).

An expedition (December 626) to the wells of
Muraisi, north of Jiddah, on the seashore resulted in
the defeat of Beni-Mustalik and the capture of a large
number of persons.   Among the captives was Juweira,
the beautiful daughter of the chief.   The prophet, quite
taken up with her beauty, ransomed her and added her
to his harem, as his eigth wife.

THE BATTLE OF OHOD

At Mecca there was a burning desire to revenge the
defeat of Badr, and they decided to take up arms
against Mahommed.   Abu Sufyan had risen to the
occasion ; he had persuaded his fellow townsmen to
devote to preparation the whole of their profit of the
year ; he had likewise some allies in the coast tribes
and the Kinanah.   He had been joined at this time
by an influential man from Medina with many followers.
Abu Sufyan had done his best to raise a sufficiently
strong force, and thus early in 625 three thousand
Koreish fighting men, the right wing commanded
by the great warrior Khalid, marched northwards.
Mahommed and his family were in the midst of their
domestic joys, when the news arrived at Medina that
a well-equipped force, thrice the size of that which had
been defeated at Badr, was on its way to retrieve that
misfortune.   Mahommed summoned his followers to
attack, promising them the aid of five thousand angels
from above ; of those who had been called to arms,
he chose one thousand strong and well disciplined
fighting men.   To encourage his troops, he made an
animated oration, in which he reminded them how
God had made him His Prophet and the channel

through which God's commands or prohibitions
were conveyed to mankind. The Prophet's force
succeeded in reaching Ohod, before the Koreisites had
perceived their tactics. Thus he secured a strong
position, and in doing so the Koreistes were placed
between his army and Medina. He stationed a de-
tachment of fifty archers on the side of a hill with
strict orders to remain there till they were told to
come down. The fight began and at the very commencement events were going as the Prophet had
imagined. The champions of Badr, Ali and Hamzah
dealt out death as unsparingly as before. Hamzah however was killed, but the slaughter on the Meccan side
was very great; several of their standard bearers and
champions were killed, which made the Meccan army
turn and fly, leaving their camp to the enemy, who at
once proceeded to pillage it. The archers who had
been posted to protect the Moslem rear came down
to join in the plunder and this gave the gallant
soldier Khalid who was commanding the right wing of
the Meccan army the chance to make a dexterous
descent with his cavalry on Mahommed's rear. This
sudden diversion checked the rout and the Moslems
found themselves caught between two fires. Discipline
could not be restored, nor was it easy to distinguish
friend from foe. Khalid, to cause greater confusion
among the followers of the Prophet, raised the cry that
Mahommed was slain, although he had only been wounded
and carried hurriedly for safety into a ravine by Ali,
where he could be tended. The Meccans who bore
no sort of ill-will to Mahommed's followers, supposing
their chief business which was to kill Mahommed had
been accomplished, did not care to proceed with the
victory. Thus the cry that Mahommed was slain rather
saved Mahommed and his cause. Had the Koreisites
preserved their original position between Medina and

the Moslems and followed the pursuit, the latter must
have been destroyed when the rout began, notwithstanding the aid of five thousand angels they had from
above. While the Meccans only lost twenty-two, more
than seventy of the Moslems were slain in the battle,
besides over seventy wounded among whom Abu
Bekr and Ali figured, but the Prophet comforted his
followers by regarding the slain as martyrs of God and
alive with Him, and quoted revelations to say that God
sometimes sends alternations of success as tests to see
the fidelity of his followers, and exhorted them to per-
severe in the new faith, even should he himself be
killed, and they should understand that no one dies
without the permission of God. Mahommed remained
in the field five days to see whether the Meccans
would return to attack Medina, but they realised
too late their folly in having left their work and
victory unfinished. Notwithstanding his wounds, the
Prophet succeeded in mounting his horse and conduct-
ing the retreat with good order. The Meccans who
had not cared to follow the pursuit, indulged themselves in the hope that so decisive a victory over
Mahommed would break the spell which enchained
the Moslems, who had now ocular demonstration that
Mahommed had no allies of a supernatural order and
that even his sacred person was not proof against
material weapons. Though this battle was disastrous
to Mahommed in several other ways, it gained to his
harem Hafsah, the daughter of his friend Omar, who
had fallen a martyr in the battle. Her father Omar
had offered her to Abu Behr and Othman, but these
persons preferred leaving her to the Prophet, who
wanted her for himself.

THE BATTLE OF THE DITCH

THE Jews, who had been forced to abandon their homes
and their fortress, were now trying hard to get others
to fight and thus to break down the power of Mahommed,
who had already suffered such a severe reverse. They
sent deputations everywhere, denouncing the impostor,
who wished to subjugate all Arabia. They succeeded
in making a treaty with the Meccans at Kaaba, by which
the parties were bound to oppose Mahommed so long as
any of them were alive. The Jews had also succeeded
in stirring up the tribes of the neighbouring provinces
of Ghatafan, Asad and Sulaim. The purpose of the
great expedition was to capture Medina and thus to
stop the mischief at its very source. In March 627 the
Jews thus allied with the Meccans and the great Bedouin
tribes, in all 10,000 strong, under Abu-Sufyan laid siege
to Medina. A certain Persian by name Salman advised
Mahommed to defend the city by a trench. This idea
of defence by a trench did not much please the Arabs,
whose notions of war were rather chivalrous than
practical. In any case, there was one side where the
buildings of Medina were not sufficiently close together
to constitute a defence. The prophet, with good sense
took a pickaxe himself, marked out the line of entrench-
ment and divided the work of digging between his three
thousand followers, who worked continuously in relays.
The women and children were meanwhile placed for
security in the towers. Mahommed entrenched himself
behind a wide ditch, and his followers defended it so
well that the invading army was quite unable to cross
it. The invaders therefore waited outside the trench
in the hope that the Moslems would come out and
fight, but when they discovered that the Moslems,
who had sufficient foodstuffs in the city, to last for
more than a year, had no intention of going out to

fight, broke up and returned home after a futile siege
of over a month during which they suffered intensely on
account of cold winter nights. This was the best and
also the last chance given to the Meccans and Jews of
breaking Mahommed's power; and it was utterly wasted,
partly for want of physical courage, but chiefly because
there was no man with brains in command. The un-
foreseen stratagem of the trench seems to have paralysed
them as completely as the machine gun might paralyse
an enemy who had never heard of gunpowder.

THE DESTRUCTION OF THE JEWS

MAHOMMED, it is said, had spent most of the time of the
siege praying, and when he learnt that his prayers had
been answered, and the invaders · had dispersed, he
would not put off his armour, before he commenced the
work of vengeance on the treacherous Kuraizah Jews,
who had been the chief instruments of this invasion.
Huyaya their chief, who had organised the original
campaign, loyally remained with the Kuraizahs in their
extremity. The Moslem force 3000 strong invaded
their stronghold and besieged their city. The Jews,
about 2000 strong, offered a stubborn resistance; and
after four weeks' siege, during which they tried in
vain to obtain some terms of peace, capitulated
apparently on condition that their fate should be
decided by a member of the Aus tribe. One Sad-Muag
who was chosen to decide their fate was in no merciful
mood and his award was a foregone conclusion. 'The
men were to be killed; their goods to be seized, and
the women and children to be enslaved; which of the
lads were to count as men and which as children was
to be determined by medical examination' was the
award pronounced by this man, and which greatly
pleased Mahommed, who accordingly ordered the

separation of men from the women and children, who were left under the charge of a strong guard; a trench was dug across the market place and 700 of the male captives were brought out in companies of six at a time and were beheaded on the brink of the trench and their bodies were cast therein. One shudders at the recital of this horrible transaction and at the picture of the man, a messenger of the most merciful God, who, unmoved to pity, nay more, with fierce denunciation, could witness this awful carnage, a deed of incomparable atrocity, to its end. This crime is not only memorable for its atrocity, but affords us a view of the sanguinary principles which at this time regulated Mahommed's conduct. Yet in the Koran this accursed slaughter is applauded, attributed to divine interposition, and pronounced as quite consonant with the love and compassion of the All-Merciful God ! Without doubt this butchery of the Kuraizah Jews leaves a dark stain of infamy on the character of Mahommed, the prophet of God. The women and children were then sold into slavery, except one, the beautiful Rainah, who was kept by Mahommed as a slave concubine. After this heartless butchery, Mahommed retired to solace himself with this captive Rainah, whose husband and near male relatives were among the massacred. Rainah, though she absolutely refused to marry with him or change her faith, had no escape from the sensuality of the Prophet of Islam.

MAHOMMED AND AYESHAH

MAHOMMED having learned that a certain Banu Mustalih of the tribe of Kuzaihah of a neighbouring province, meditated a raid on Medina, attacked their city capturing two thousand camels, five thousand sheep and two hundred women, among whom was

E

Barrah a daughter of the chieftain, and a woman of great beauty, who was added at once to his harem to consummate his victory.

The prophet, who soon found it difficult to keep the peace in his harem, had adopted the plan of letting his wives draw lots among themselves for the honour of accompanying him on his expeditions, and to Ayeshah the lot had fallen on this occasion. Ayeshah who was just fifteen years old, was a great favourite of the prophet. Her haughty ill-nature at the same time had also made her many enemies. After the expedition when the army was starting homeward, Ayeshah who had dropped her necklace in the sand, had stopped behind with a youth named Safwan, to make a search for the missing jewel. Why evil should have been thought of what seems a perfectly natural occurrence, one cannot say. The supposed delinquency of Ayeshah was greedily seized on by a number of persons. One Hassan began to circulate infamous verses against her, and the notorious Ali who bore a secret hatred towards her even recommended her divorce to the prophet. When she was asked openly by the prophet (who had now begun to treat her with marked disfavour) in the presence of her father Abu Bekr, she indignantly refused to answer. Mahommed was now in considerable perplexity: if he believed her to be guilty it would discredit Abu Bekr her father and his own most faithful friend and benefactor, and she, his favourite wife, would have to be subjected to the same law by which other persons guilty of the like crime were judged. Would this horrible fate then really befall the blooming girl, who claimed the premiership in the harem, and who even made the prophet feel that he was her father's debtor? It was a very dark cloud, and the prophet had recourse to a revelation; he covered himself up and presently exhibited himself in a violent state of perspiration. A revelation came down and the Angel Gabriel made known to Mahommed the will of heaven. God the Almighty declared Ayeshah innocent; the queenly Ayeshah in all her dignity told her husband that she thanked God, but owed him no thanks. Mahommed thereupon protested against the conduct of those who had entertained such suspicion against this his innocent wife even for a moment; and severe chastisements were administered to the gossip mongers and to those who had the hardihood to meddle in the prophet's domestic affairs. He further ruled that the prophet's privacy was in no way in future to be disturbed by gossiping tongues. He also made the law that a charge of adultery against a woman must be substantiated by four witnesses, and that a false accusation of this kind should be dealt very seriously, such as scourging with four score stripes.

MAHOMMED VISITS MECCA

THE fact that Medina was not safe from internal foes suggested to the prophet to take some steps in the direction of regaining Mecca. In the month of March 628 he determined to attempt a pilgrimage and enter the sacred mosque of Mecca. Accordingly he issued a proclamation to the Arabs round Medina, inviting them to accompany him on this sacred expedition, hoping thereby to impress upon them the fact that he was bent on maintaining the national religion. About 1500 responded to his call and prepared to start with him. They started accordingly, taking a number of camels for sacrifice which were decorated according to custom; meanwhile hearing that the Meccans with a large force were prepared to oppose his entry and even had sent the gallant soldier Khalid with two hundred horsemen in advance to check his progress,

Mahommed changed his route and halted at Hudabeya some eight miles from Mecca. Though Mahommed did not intend storming Mecca, still under the pretence of the pilgrimage, he was not unwilling to impress the Meccans with a sense of his might, and wealth and the reverence and awe which he inspired. The Koreisites sent a messenger to know what Mahommed wanted and to express their determination not to let him inside the sacred city whether he came as a friend or as an enemy. Mahommed took care that this man saw the sacrificial camels and the uncombed pilgrims; Hulais the messenger affected by the sight urged the Meccans to compromise with their unwelcome visitors. Meantime Mahommed sent Othman as his representative to the Meccans to persuade his former townmen that he really meant no harm and that there was now an opportunity for both the communities to make a treaty for some years, since both had suffered so much from this continued warfare. In the interval the followers of the prophet, made a solemn league, under a tree, holding a branch of it over the prophet, vowing not to turn their backs should they be forced to fight. The Meccans were even more ready for a compromise, and sent as their plenipotentiaries to Mahommed, Arwa Musad the prince of the tribe of Thakif, and Suhail a man famed as an orator. A truce or treaty was concluded between them for ten years, by which Mahommed and his party were to turn back that year without making the pilgrimage but in the following years full liberty was to be accorded them to perform the pilgrimage, for which purpose Mecca was to be evacuated for three days and freedom was given to all either to join the faith of Islam or to remain in the religion of the Koreisites. The terms of this treaty made his followers, especially Omar, blush with shame but Mahommed made a triumph of it and called it

'Victory in the Vale of Mecca' saying that bloodshed was only prevented by divine interposition. The Koreisites were now growing proud of their kinsman and were beginning to pay him in his own country the honour which was lavished on him elsewhere. Indeed, deep and inconceivable was the respect and veneration that was lavished on the prophet by his followers. Arwa Musad the above named plenipotentiary attests, that though he had been present in the courts of Roman and Persian Emperors, he had never seen any prince so deeply and highly venerated by his subjects as Mahommed was by his followers, for whenever the prophet made ablutions in order to say prayers the people would run to catch the water he had used for that purpose, and whenever he spat, his followers out of veneration to the relic of his sacred person, would lick it up, and they would gather carefully every hair that would fall from his body and would preserve the same as a most precious relic.

MAHOMMED AND THE KHAIBAR JEWS

EACH time the prophet had failed or scored an incomplete success, he compensated for it by an attack on the Jews, and such a policy had served too well to be abandoned after the unsatisfactory affair of Hodobeyah. Therefore Mahommed after his return from Mecca turned his arms against the rich Jews of Khaibar, which was a famous and very rich village in the province of Hejaz north of Medina. Mahommed by this time knew the Jews too well to fear however strong their fortification might be, and so he took with him only those who had accompanied him to Hodobeyah, though several others expressed their willingness to share in this expedition. The Jews of Khaibar defended themselves very well, and the Moslem army after a siege of over two

months was about to retire for want of food, when
some traitors revealed to Mahommed where the siege
machinery was hidden and where the forts were weak,
and he thus was enabled to overcome and subdue
these brave Jews.   Mahommed however this time was
a little more politic, he did not want to destroy this
fine village nor banish its industrious inhabitants,
but he levied a very heavy tax of half of their annual
produce which was estimated to be about two hundred
thousand wasks of dates.   Thus the Jews of Khaiber
were to be the first subject race, whose lives were to be
guaranteed but whose earnings were to go to the support
of the true believers.   The taking of Khaibar was also
marked by two other events.   One Huyaya a most
earnest adversary among the Jews of the prophet was
assassinated by Mahommed's order.   His daughter
Safiyah had been married to Kinanah the chief of
Khaibar who also was tortured to death during the
taking of the Khaibar.   Mahommed's greediness was
now excited by the report that some very rich silver and
gold vessels and other treasures were concealed in the
house of Safiyah.   He therefore lost no time in looting
the house of Safiyah who was then about sixteen
years old and carried her away captive.   One of the
followers of Mahommed begged her for himself, but
the Prophet of the Islam struck with her beauty, threw
his mantle over her and took her to his harem to become
his bride and the wedding was celebrated by a feast.

We have already seen how Mahommed had become
deeply and irreconcileably hostile to the Jews, and
though at first he had availed himself of their aid to
establish himself at Medina, when success enabled him
to slight their assistance, he threw them contemptuously
aside and eagerly availed himself of any plausible
excuse for their destruction.   In addition his dark
suspicions were aroused that a lingering illness which

troubled him was due to certain *enchantments*, which
the Jews had directed against him : The 113th Sura
is a short prayer to God for deliverance from 'the
mischief of the night when it cometh on and from the
mischief of women blowing on knots, etc.' We may
gather from this prayer some knowledge of the superstitious fears and that dread of the Unseen, which
formed so curious a feature in the complex character of
Mahommed. In accordance with the prophet's belief
in magic, incantations etc., the use of charms, and
amulets is universal among Mahometans, to counteract
the influence of enchantments, disease, the evil eye, etc.
Of these charms, the most potent is a copy of the Koran ;
but the faithful as a rule content themselves with certain
verses only, invoking God's protection against the devil.
The texts are written out and enclosed in amulets, and
worn on the neck or arm. Bits of the 'Kiswa' or silken
covering of the Kaaba, which is renewed annually, are
considered very efficacious.

MAHOMMED POISONED

ZAINAB a Jewess, who had lost her husband Sallam and
several other relatives during the siege of Khaibar and
had been kept as a female slave concubine by the
prophet, planned a frightful revenge ; she watched
what joint was the Prophet's choicest food and accordingly she dressed a kid and having steeped it in poison,
placed the dish with fair words before the prophet for
his evening repast. Mahommed gratefully accepting the
gift, took for himself his favourite piece, the shoulder, and
distributed other portions to Abu Bekr and his other
friends who were seated with him at supper. No sooner
had Mahommed put the first piece in his mouth, than
he spat it out, crying 'Hold, this has been poisoned.'
One who had meantime swallowed a piece of the meat

died instantly, and Mahommed himself was seized with
excruciating pains. When Zainab was put on her
defence for this heinous crime, she said 'Thou hast in-
flicted injuries on my people and hast slain my husband
and my father ; therefore said I within myself, " If he be
a Prophet of God, he will reject the gift knowing that
it has been poisoned, but if he be only a pretender, we
shall be thus rid of our troubles." '

MAHOMMED AND NEIGHBOURING CHIEFS

THE vast spoils of Khaibar now enabled the prophet
to abundantly enrich his wives, his concubines, his
daughters and their offspring. Moreover, there was no
fear of this wealth melting away, for the Jews had
remained back at Khaibar a subject race to till the
land whose produce was to support Mahommed and his
followers. The news of the victory of the Khaibar
alarmed the neighbouring provinces of Fadak, Wadial,
Kura and Taima, and the people of these provinces sent
to the prophet half of their produce before he came and
took away their all, and submitted themselves as a
subject race like the Jews of Khaibar. The prophet
gladly accepted it, for thus the whole profit fell to his
share, since it had been won without the sword.

The prophet's weakness and the object of his secret
amusements and pleasures being generally known
everywhere, fair women were sent to him from various
parts ; and indeed at Medina whenever a young and fair
woman became a widow, her relations would not find
her a husband before asking whether the prophet
wanted her.

MAHOMMED AND THE GREAT POWERS

THE taking of Khaibar marks the stage at which Islam
became a menace to the whole world. Mahommed for the

last six years had lived by robbery and brigandage; in plundering the Meccans he could plead that he and his followers had been driven away from their homes and possessions, and with the Jews of Medina he had some real or pretended outrage to avenge; but the Jews of Khaibar living so far distant had done no wrong to the prophet or his followers. When Ali, who had been ordered to take the standard and the forces against Khaibar, had asked of the prophet for what he was fighting with these Jews, he was peremptorily told ' To compel those Jews to accept the religion of Islam,'—a fine excuse for attack, when a large booty was to be acquired there; a plea that would cover attacks on the whole world outside Medina and its neighbourhood. The prophet on leaving Khaibar, perhaps was meditating how to bring the whole world under his grasp.

In the seventh year of the Hejira (628) therefore, Mahommed published his intention of propagating his religion beyond the boundaries of Arabia and for this purpose he sent messengers to the neighbouring kings and princes with letters to invite them to embrace the religion of Islam. He sent an envoy, April 628, to the victorious Byzantine Emperor Heraclius, to say that he should acknowledge Mahommed as an apostle of God, and laying aside the worship of Jesus, that he should embrace the faith of Islam. The Emperor, it is said, received the envoy with marked respect and sent him back honourably. Mahommed at the same time sent also a similar message to Khosru Parviz, King of Persia, who, however, received the envoy disdainfully, tore the letter to pieces and ordered the governor of Yeman to bring him bound the man who dared to send such a letter to his Suzarain. The news of this order caused great joy to the inhabitants of Arabia, but before it was executed Khosru Parviz died and Badham who was then governor of Yeman not

caring to execute the order of his defunct king, himself
with many Persians embraced the faith of Islam.   The
embassy sent to Muckonkas the Roman governor of
Egypt, was received very favourably and the governor
in return sent several valuable presents to Mahommed,
including two Coptic girls, one of whom named Mary
was immediately added to his harem and became a
great favourite, nay one who went near perpetuating
the prophet's dynasty, as we shall see hereafter.   Mahommed also sent letters of the like purport to several
Arab princes, namely to the kings of Ghassan, of
Yamama and of Bhahrein, who all sooner or later
embraced Islamism more or else on political grounds.
The King of Abyssinia is reported to have also joined
the new religion about this time.

MAHOMMED VISITS MECCA

THE time for the execution of the Prophet's project of
a pilgrimage to Mecca had come according to the terms
of the treaty of Hodobeyah.   He had now all the dignity
and position of a royal personage.   He had moreover
taken into his harem as his eleventh wife, Umma
Habibah the widow of one of his followers and the
daughter of Abu Sufyn the staunch leader of the
Meccans and the prophet's arch-enemy.   Mecca according to the terms of the treaty was to be evacuated by the
Koreisites for three days.   Accordingly in March 629
Mahommed with 2000 followers and with 200 horsemen
which he took for any case of emergency, started to
Mecca on pilgrimage.   They had the Kaaba to themselves for three days.   Mahommed seated on his camel,
the famous Al Caswa, which eight years ago had borne
him on his flight from Mecca, approached the Kaaba,
touched the black stone with his staff very reverently,
after which he made the customary seven circuits round

the holy house, and then performed the prayers and other devotions according to the rites of the new religion and then the sixty camels that had been decorated and brought in procession were slain as victims. During his short stay at Mecca the prophet found time for a diversion from more serious matters and he arranged for yet another marriage, with Maimunah a beautiful young widow, his uncle Abbas acting as bride's guardian. The marriage took place at Saif some eight miles from Mecca ; this was his twelfth and last regular marriage.

The spectacle of this pilgrimage produced two important conversions to Islam from among the Meccans ; the one that of the famous soldier Khalid the hero of Ohod who rather than bear the humiliation of seeing Moslems enter into and desecrate the holy temple of Kaaba, himself went out of Mecca and embraced the new religion. This new convert became afterwards still more famous by bringing Syria under the command of Mahommed and was named on that account the 'Sword of Allah.' The other conversion was that of Amru another very skilful soldier who helped the prophet to bring Egypt under the banner of Islam.

MAHOMMED TAKES MECCA

At the close of 629 Mahommed, desirous of making himself master of Mecca and as an excuse alleging some infractions of the terms of the treaty of Hodobeyah by the Meccans, mustured an army of about 10,000 troops, and though Abu Sufyan the leader of the Meccans at the head of a deputation journied to Medina with a view of healing the supposed breach of terms of the treaty and most humbly asked of the prophet to renew the truce ; Mahommed received the distinguished suppliant with sardonic smiles and made him return to his people with the knowledge that their long rivalry with the Prophet of Islam was nearing its termination. Mahommed wishing to conceal his purpose from the Meccans, steadily proceeded towards Mecca to take it by surprise. The Meccans, though they were unprepared to meet so formidable an army, still offered some resistence. Abu Sufyan at the head of a scouting party met the prophet's army outside the city, but being persuaded by Abbas that it was not too late for him to save his head and property as well as the lives of many of his friends by the profession of his faith in the prophet's mission, resigned himself to this humiliation not without reluctance, acknowledging that his gods had been defeated by Mahommed's God and therefore that he owed the former no further allegiance. Before Mahommed could enter the city there were several skirmishes here and there between the Meccans and the cavalry under the command of the new convert Khalid with slight losses on both sides ; about twenty-eight of the Meccans were killed and the remainder surrendered at discretion. Now Mecca was won for the prophet. Mahommed greatly delighted at the unconditional surrender of the Meccans entered the city triumphantly with his army and immediately going into the Kaaba, saluted the sacred stone and performed the seven circuits round the temple and said the prayers. The idols, which had roused the prophet's scorn and to which he owed his banishment, were now utterly destroyed. The great idol of Hobal that stood in front of the Kaaba was broken to pieces and the paintings of Abraham and of the angels that adorned the interior walls of the Kaaba were effaced. He moreover gave orders to all believers to destroy forthwith all the idols and pictures that were in their houses. The Koreish finding that every opposition and all attempts to put down Mahommed were in vain,

now with one mind made their submission to the
prophet, who was very much delighted to see all his
countrymen the Koreish embrace the new religion and
acknowledge him to be the great prophet of Allah.
He ordered all the pillars marking the boundaries
of the sacred place to be repaired, thus showing his
intention to maintain the sanctity of Mecca. He said
that the sanctity of the Kaaba was to suffer no diminution by the religious innovations, the more important
ceremonies were to remain as before, and he refused
to touch the vast treasures of over seventy thousand
ounces of gold that were in the Kaaba. The prophet's
stay at Mecca was not very long, as he was anxious to
assure his friends of Medina that he had no intention
of leaving them for his former home, of which indeed
there was some danger, since he did not conceal his
opinion that Mecca was the best spot on earth and
the dearest of all places to God. Mahommed before
leaving Mecca appointed Ahib as governor of Mecca
on a fixed salary; this was the first permanent civil
appointment made in Islam. Besides the civil governor
he made Muad son of Jabal of Medina the spiritual
officer, to teach the Meccans the new religion and to
conduct prayers and services. After thus settling
the affairs of Mecca the prophet returned to Medina
in triumph.

MAHOMMED AND THE GREEKS

AMONG the letters sent out by Mahommed at the time
when he felt it his duty to summon all mankind to
follow his doctrine, was one addressed to the governor
of Bostra subject to the Byzantine Emperor. The envoy
had been disdainfully sent away by the governor and
on his return journey was slain on the way by an
Arab at Balka in Syria, also said to be an official in the

Emperor's pay. Mahommed to avenge the death of the
messenger sent by him on such a holy errand, soon
mustered a force 3000 strong and sent it against the
governor of Bostra, without reflecting that he was
running the risk of war against the unlimited forces
of the great Emperor. Perhaps he regarded this as
one of the many raids on Arabic or Jewish tribes
which kept his treasury full. Zaid, a not unsuccessful
leader of raids, was chosen to command, and Khalid was
appointed the next in rank. The Grecian army vastly
superior in number repulsed the attack of the Moslems,
who lost in the fight three of their best generals,
Zaid the chief commander and the adopted son of
Mahommed, Zaafer the Prophet's cousin, and Abdullah.
The whole Moslem army would have been annihilated,
had not the gallant hero Khalid come to their aid
in time and taken the command of the army, rally-
ing together with great tact and dexterity the broken
forces, which in the end overthrew the Grecian
forces with great slaughter and brought back a great
abundance of rich spoil to Mahommed, who in recognition of the valuable services of the gallant soldier
Khalid conferred on him the honourable title of ' Seif
min Soyuf Allah ' meaning one of the Swords of God.
Likewise high honours in Paradise were awarded
by the grateful Prophet to all who had fallen in this
battle, especially to his once adopted son Zaid, whose
death was perhaps not without its consolation and relief
since he was so closely connected with one of the worst
scandals of the Prophet's domestic life.

BATTLE OF HONAIN

MANY of the Arab tribes seeing Mahommed was everywhere victorious and that the Koreish, the chief tribe
of the whole Arab nation and the genuine descendants

of Ishmael had quietly made their submission to the Prophet, thought it wise not to oppose him further and they began to make their submission, in great numbers and in this manner wisely averted war against themselves. The Hawazin and Thakifite tribes who lived in the neighbourhood of Mecca, under their chief Auf Malik however determined to make a bold stand against the raids of Mahommed ; who on the other hand resolved to subdue them and with a large force of 12,000 strong attacked the united tribes in the valley of Hunain in February 630 A.D. The united forces of the tribes of Hawazin and Thakif about 5000 strong speedily entered the valley and attacked the enemy on all sides, the shower of their arrows with which these tribes were skilled marksmen, doing havoc among the Moslem army, composed in great part of discontented new converts, who seeing the brave defence, at first turned back in headlong confusion. But the Prophet conscious of the fact that a defeat in the neighbourhood of Mecca, so long obstinate and so recently overcome, would mean a disaster of very great magnitude, reminded the fugitives of their solemn pledges and their glorious victories and did his best to encourage them. Thus animated the heroes of Badr gathered round the Prophet and stemming the rout, attacked the enemy with renewed vigour and won the day. Mahommed ascribed the victory won with a force 12,000 strong stimulated to fanaticism, over an army only 5000 strong, to the aid of unseen angelic hosts. This victory of Hunain, like that of Badr was considered worthy of mention in the Koran and Mahommed even considered this victory the more important because as the defeat of the Koreisites was commenced at Badr, so it was consummated at Honain. This victory is thus alluded to in the Koran, ' God hath assisted you in many engagements and at the battle of Honain, when ye pleased yourselves with your multitude, but it was no manner of advantage unto you—then did ye retreat and turn your backs. Afterwards God sent His security (Shechina) upon His apostle and upon the faithful, and sent down troops of angels which ye saw not' (Sura ix. 25, 26).

After the victory of Honain it was the prophet's desire to take Taef the headquarters of the Hawzain and Thakfite tribes, a city then supposed to be a store of vast riches. Its soil is very fertile and it is famous for its orchards and the cultivation of the vine. Mahommed accordingly after the battle of Honain, laid siege to Taef, but the Thakifites, notwithstanding that their former leader Auf Malik to save his life had embraced Islam, after his defeat at Honain, so boldly and valiantly withstood the siege, that after forty days of persistence in the siege, Mahommed considered it advisable to raise it and abandon the project of subduing the Thakfites. The Moslems no longer objected to the order for retreat and the brave resistance of the Thakfites even extorted some compliment from those Moslems whose nature had not been changed entirely by the new religion. It will be remembered that in the very beginning of his apostolic mission, Mahommed had visited this idolatrous city, and had been driven away from its walls ; and now again the strength of its fortifications and its ample resources enabled it to defy all his efforts, though he was victorious and triumphant in every other place.

The distribution of the booty from Honain, which was particularly rich on account of the folly of the Hawazins who had brought their families and possessions into the battlefield, caused much dissatisfaction among the Medina men, because great favour was shown to the Meccans, especially to Abu Sufyan ; but Mahommed again appeased them by expressing his unchangeable gratitude to them and his determination to remain by them as against all the world.

HAWAZINS AND SHAKIFITES SUBMIT

MEDINA was now in the position of the capital of an
Empire, sending out rulers to subject tribes and tax
gatherers to collect tribute. The return of the Prophet
to his capital from his expeditions was always marked
with triumph and Mahommed on such occasions, was
not backward in displaying the extent of his riches and
the magnitude of his power. About this time Arwa,
the hero of Thaif, who had so stubbornly resisted the
siege by Mahommed and compelled him to raise it of his
own accord, came to Medina and tendered his submission
and embraced the new faith. This conversion brightened
the hopes of Mahommed of subjugating the powerful
and heroic Shakifites. The desertion of their heroic
leader and the persistent raids of the Moslems, which
compelled the Shakifites to keep within their walls, soon
forced them to send an embassy to Medina to arrange a
compromise. Mahommed gladly received the deputation
and accepted their submission on their conforming to the
new religion and abandoning their idol worship, which
they had to do to save their lives and property.
Mahommed deputed Abu Sufyan to destroy the famous
idol Al Lat, which was done amid the lamentations
of their women and children. The money and jewels,
appropriate to the service of the idol were seized by
Abu Sufyan on behalf of the Prophet. Othman, son
of Abu Asi, a young man, was appointed governor
of the new province of Shakifites and he was instructed
not to be too exigent in the matter of the ceremonies of
Islam with the newly converted Shakifites. They were
also relieved of the obligation of giving legal alms and
of going to battle.

MAHOMMED AND CHRISTIANS

MAHOMMED'S dominion now began to assume the pro-
portions of an Empire. Embassies were received from

F

all parts of Arabia and even beyond, acknowledging
Mahommed's leadership and paying him annual
tribute which was exacted by force where necessary.
Unlike most of the Embassies was that from the
Christian state of Nazran. This community of Arabian
Christians sent a deputation to Medina, believing that
the Prophet would welcome them as co-religionists and
even called themselves Islamists, because they argued
that Mahommed had such a regard and esteem to
Jesus Christ, whom he called a great Prophet as well
as to the Blessed Virgin Mary, whose Virgin Birth he
accepted and respected, that his view and doctrines
would not differ essentially from their own and even if
it did differ, some compromise could be arrived at.
But Mahommed knew enough about Christianity and
he refused either to recognise them as Islamists or
condescend to any compromise. There were enough
persons at Medina to tell these Christians what disasters
had fallen on the Jews, who had refused to acknowledge
Mahommed as their Prophet and if they were unable to hold their own against the forces of the
Moslems their submission was advisable. At the
threats of danger these staunch Christians chose
rather to defy the Prophet than to abandon
their religion and become followers of Mahommed.
This refusal of the Christians to acknowledge him as
their Prophet, left in his mind no less bitterness
against them than he had harboured against the Jews.
He appointed a fanatical Moslem by name Abu Ubaidah
as the governor over this Christian state of Nazran
and heavy taxes were levied on them. Mahommed
declared that the Christians of Nazran as well as those
of Taglibit, who had also acted like their brethren of
Nazran, were the two worst tribes of Arabia, and that
Christians and Jews would serve as substitutes for
Moslems in hell fire. The Christian tribes who had

thus submitted to his secular power by paying the tribute were allowed for a time to continue in their religion, but he forbade the baptism of their children. In 630 he sent an expedition against the Christians and Jews that inhabited south of Palestine and forced them to embrace Islam.

THE BAN AGAINST UNBELIEVERS

THE year 631 was marked by an important event in the history of Islam : the first pilgrimage over which a Moslem official presided. Mahommed being very busily engaged in some domestic affairs, deputed his bosom friend Abu Bekr to perform the pilgrimage to Mecca with 300 pilgrims. Hitherto the heathen tribes had been permitted to visit Mecca and to perform their idolatrous rites here. A manifesto or order was now sent with Abu Bekr for proclamation to all Arabs that in future the pilgrimage to the sanctuary of the Kaaba would be limited only to the Believers in Allah and no unbeliever would be allowed in future to take part in the pilgrimage nor to approach the sacred place of Kaaba. The crime of keeping people from God's house, which had been very serious when the Meccans had the power over the Kaaba, now assumed a different aspect when the Apostle of God became master over it. He moreover sent orders to his governors that the churches of the Christians and the synagogues of the Jews should be demolished everywhere and that mosques should be erected on their sites. He likewise sent out various officers to different places with authority and powers both to instruct the heathen and to convert them to the religion Islam, as well as to collect taxes and administer justice according to the rules and regulations laid down in the Koran.

MAHOMMED AND HIS DOMESTIC TROUBLES

MAHOMMED's harem had now become too numerous to be easily governed. The battle of Badr had first given him the means of establishing a princely harem. We have seen how year after year he had been adding new wives to his harem. Every important battle or expedition brought to him among the spoils some woman of rare beauty whom he eagerly made one of his wives or concubines. His taste and the secret of his pleasures being generally known, we have likewise seen how tribes anxious to gain his favour, presented him with the fairest of their women, most of whom were added to his harem or kept as concubines; and how Mahommed to keep peace among his jealous wives, had hit upon the idea of casting lots among them to decide which was to accompany him in his expeditions. The spirit of jealousy and rivalry grew very strong among the wives. His relations with Mary the Coptic girl who had been sent him by the governor of Egypt, gave great offence to the other wives, owing to the Prophet's evident partiality for her. His relations with several of his wives had become of a ceremonial and formal nature. Mary was his favourite wife, in her company he spent most of his time. The daughter of his friend Omar, Hafsah, whom he had married after the death of her husband at Ohodi for political reasons was a woman of violent temper, and finding her rights endangered by the favour shown to the favourite wife Mary made many complaints. Ayeshah the blooming young girl, daughter of his bosom friend Abu Bekr, whose purity and innocence had been declared by heaven, could not bear the Prophet's preference for this Coptic girl, as she claimed the premiership in the harem, because she was the daughter of the Prophet's greatest benefactor. Tainab the wife of his adopted son Zaid, and whose marriage with the Prophet had caused the greatest scandal among his followers, though it was sanctioned by a special revelation from heaven, claimed on this account some special privilege over his other wives and resented his too great attachment to the Coptic girl, as also did his daughter Fatima, who though married to Ali, was living for the most part with her father giving no room for scandal.

Hafsah at the head of the discontented wives revolted. Mahommed resolved to leave his harem and threatened to divorce all his wives, producing revelation in the manner characteristic of his later life to suit the case, showing that heaven approved of his conduct. He then declared that he gave the option to his wives of quitting him, if they wished, and Ayeshah declining the offer, at the head of his wives, sought pardon of the Prophet. Khadijah, Mahommed's first wife, who had paved the way for his future fortune, and who was the only wife during her life time, had borne him two sons who died young and four daughters, of whom the most famous was the above said Fatima ; but after her death, though he had taken so many wives and concubines, they were all childless, except the Coptic girl Mary, who had given birth to a son, of whom Mahommed claimed to be the father, his fatherhood being attested by the infant's features, though the rival wives especially the astute Ayeshah and the zealous Hafsah could not trace the resemblance in the infant. Mahommed made a great feast at Medina, to celebrate the birth of his only son, to whom he gave the name of Ibrahim the name of the mythical founder of his religion ; but unfortunately the boy died sixteen months afterwards—it is suspected from causes not unknown to some of the jealous wives. The death of his son caused very great grief to the Prophet, because he fondly trusted that the child might be destined to transmit his name to posterity, but now these hopes were frustrated and with a broken heart he followed the beloved remains to the cemetery of El-Bakia. No spot more sacred than this is visited by the devout pilgrim to Medina ; because in this cemetery, lie, with the exception of Khadijah, all the prophet's wives, the ' mothers of the Faithful,' and here there are the tombs of Othman, the third Caliph, of Abbas the prophet's beloved uncle, of Halima the prophet's nurse, of three of his daughters, of Hasan his murdered grandson, as well as of numberless martyrs, princes and imams.

MAHOMMED CHANGES HIS POLICY

MAHOMMED, whose glory, power, wealth was at its zenith, now changed his policy, so as not to disturb the existing order of affairs. The chieftains and princes, who gave in their submission to Islam were confirmed in their rights and their old titles were retained. The Prophet merely sent back with them an official whose business was to collect the Alms from the Believers and the tribute from the unbelievers like the Jews and the Christians, who were left to follow their own religion ; and another official who was to instruct the new converts in the religion of Islam, and to conduct the religious services and to recite the Koran.

MAHOMMED'S LAST PILGRIMAGE

EARLY in 632 Mahommed made immense preparations for the great and as it happened to be, the last pilgrimage to Mecca. He set out on 17 Feb. 632 with great solemnity, accompanied by a vast multitude of his followers, including his entire harem, and with a hundred camels decorated and destined for the sacrifice. He now found mosques to pray at the several stages of his journey and in them he led public worship. When he arrived in sight of the Kaaba, he raised his hands to heaven, praising God and invoking His blessings on the pilgrims. Then he performed the several circuits and the rites preparatory to the sacrifice. He took this opportunity of fixing for ever the ceremonies and rites connected with the different places. The first day of the great pilgrimage, he delivered a solemn address to the assembly in the sanctuary of Kaaba. The subjects of the lecture being the doctrine of the brotherhood of Islam; pride in one's ancestry was forbidden since all who adopted Islam became equal or only differentiated by their piety; the world was to begin afresh, and no pre-Islamic feud was to be permitted to continue; the private property of each one was to be respected no less than his life and the women should receive humane treatment. The next day he went up to the top of the hill of Arafat and consecrated it as a pilgrimage station and recited there several parts of the Koran concluding with these words, 'This day have I perfected your religion unto you and fulfilled my mercy upon you and appointed Islam for you to be your religion.' He returned in the evening and on the way at Mozdalifa said the evening prayers. The next day he proceeded to Mina, a short distance from Mecca and there shouting the pilgrim's cry 'Labbeik, Labbeik, Labbeik' cast stones according to ancient custom at the projecting heights of the narrow valley to drive away the devils; then shaving his head and paring his nails, he slew the victims brought for sacrifice in procession and distributed the flesh for food among the pilgrims and a grand feast was held. Next day he returned to Mecca and once again made the seven circuits round the Kaaba and then, drinking the sacred waters of the famous well of Zem-Zem, he delivered the celebrated parting dis course repeating almost the same injunctions as he had done in the previous discourse. Taking off his-shoes he next went into the Kaaba and prayed for a long time at that place, and then very reverently kissing the black stone, he came out and laid aside the pilgrim garb.

At this time he conceived the unhappy idea of altering the calendar ignorant as he was of the elements of astronomy or even of the purposes of the year. Previously the months have been made to correpond roughly to the seasons ; but Mahommed on the contrary by making the year of twelve lunar months destroyed all relations between them ; and thus while desiring to fix the month of pilgrimage for the future, he greatly injured the commerce of Mecca. Having thus most rigorously performed all the ceremonies of the greater Pilgrimage as a model for all succeeding time, he then with the same triumph returned to Medina.

MAHOMMED'S LAST YEAR

THOUGH the death of his only son, whose survival and consequent claim to the direct succession would have caused serious complication in the realm of Islam, had greatly weighed down the spirits of the Prophet, even making him dismiss one of his wives for having dared to say that if the father of the child had been a Prophet, the child would not have died —a remarkable exercise of reasoning, he still found continual domestic felicity in his other wives and especially in his grand children, the family of Ali and Fatima. We have seen that Fatima the Prophet's youngest daughter was married to his cousin Ali and it was through this, his youngest daughter, that his race was to be perpetuated. Within twelve months after her marriage to Ali, she gave birth to a son whom she named Hasan. It was said that this boy's features very much resembled those of his grandfather's. Within another year she give birth to another son, called

Husain. Mahommed loved Hasan and Husain and regarded them as his own sons and many stories are told illustrative of his affection for them. The relations between Fatima and her husband Ali do not seem to have been of the most peaceful description, and she passed the greater part of her time with her father, giving no little room for scandal and for the jealousy of of the wives of the Prophet.

Besides these lineal descendants, there were many nephews, grand nephews, and cousins, about the Prophet's house, and pleasing stories are told of the games the Prophet used to play with them. When Mohammed prostrated himself in prayer, his grandchildren Hasan or Husain would sometimes mount upon their grandfather's back, or when the Prophet was standing, his grandchild would plant his knee upon his grandfather's and climb up to his breast, without in the least reflecting that their grandfather was the most sacred person, the great Prophet of Allah. At times the Prophet would appear in public with one of his grandsons on each shoulder and legend makes the holy family consist of Mahommed, Fatima and the two boys. The nephews and cousins who had arrived at manhood were the foremost claimants for the honourable post of governorships in the new administration.

The last year of Mahommed's life was chiefly occupied in receiving deputations from these peoples who were anxious to gain his friendship. After the defeat of the Hawazians, the greater number of Arabian chieftains hastened to submit to the new power. For centuries their Suzerain had been Byzantine or Persian, by a change of masters; the change was likely to be to their advantage, and probably they considered it more honourable to be under a Suzerain of their own nationality and one whose language was Arabic.

Mohammed was thus now Suzerain over the whole of Arabia, Syria and Egypt.

Amid all his duties as general, legislator, judge, and diplomatist, the Prophet did not neglect the duties of preacher and teacher. Religious controversies and some other subjects were forbidden, questions that savoured of metaphysics or rationalism were diligently excluded, because, he said, infinite mischief is done to religion by such considerations or disputes.

MAHOMMED'S LAST ILLNESS AND DEATH

THE journey from Mecca back to Medina after the last farewell pilgrimage appears to have been more than the Prophet's strength could support. The death of his son Ibrahim had weighed down his spirits, and the disturbance and disputes caused by his wives and their mutual jealousy and other domestic troubles greatly harassed him. Besides, there still remained the after effects of the poison given him by his concubine slave Zainab. A short time after his return from Medina signs of serious illness began to manifest themselves. It would appear that his mind became somewhat unhinged by fever; at dead of night a fit took him to go out to the cemetery called El-Bahia and ask forgiveness of the dead who were buried there. His faithful slave Abu Muwaihibah who had followed his master thither, saw the Prophet raise his hands to heaven and in a lengthy prayer intercede for the dead. On his way back, the Prophet related to his attendant, that God had offered him the choice either to continue his Apostolic work in this life for some years more and then enter into the glory of Paradise or to go at once to Paradise to meet and enjoy the Lord ; and that he had chosen the latter. He then spent the rest of the night restlessly wandering to and fro about the various

apartments of his wives, till he collapsed in the chamber
of his wife Maimunah, whence he begged to be transferred to the chamber of his favourite wife Ayeshah.
He now began to grow rapidly weaker and was
attacked with a violent fever. He called his wives
around him and told them that he was no more able to
visit them in turn, but that he would remain the
remainder of his days in the chamber of Ayeshah,
whither they were to come to see him. For a week
more his fever permitted him to attend the mosque and
feebly to lead the public services. Finally he publicly
announced his approaching death, at which his friend
Abu Bekr burst into tears, whereupon Mahommed
consoled him, saying to the people who were crowding
the mosque in their anxiety, 'Verily for love and
devotion to me Abu Bekr is the foremost among you
all; if I were to choose a bosom friend it would be
Abu Bekr, but Islam hath made a closer brotherhood
amongst us all.' Next day Abu Bekr was deputed to
lead prayers by the Prophet in his stead. Mahommed's
pains and sufferings now began to increase greatly
and he declared that his sins were being expiated
by his physical agonies. He then gave orders that his
tomb should not be made an object of worship saying,
'O Lord, let not my tomb be an object of worship,' and
then murmured, 'O my soul, why seekest thou for
refuge elsewhere than in God alone?' Meantime a
number of his grief-stricken followers had gathered in
the room to see for the last time their dying Prophet
and Mahommed beholding them, with great effort
spoke these last words to them : 'Verily I say to you, no
man can lay hold on me in any matter. I have not made
lawful anything but what God hath made lawful; nor
have I prohibited anything but what God hath prohibited.' After this his strength failed rapidly.
Ayeshah seeing this raised his head from the pillow,

and placed it on her breast. Realising his end was
close at hand, the Prophet asked for water, and wetting
his face and eyes made this last prayer : ' O Lord
I beseech Thee, assist me in the agonies of death, come
close O Gabriel to me,' and then in a very feeble voice :
' Lord grant me pardon and join me to the companion-
ship on high,' and stretching himself gently a little,
the Prophet of Arabia surrounded by his sorrowing
wives and grieving friends and followers, breathed his
last in the room of his favourite wife Ayeshah, at
Medina, on Monday a little after mid-day of 8th June
632, at the age of sixty-two years and after an Apostolic
and warlike life of ten years.

It is noticeable how the natural magnanimity of
his character distinctly asserts itself at the end, forming
a pleasing contrast to the unscrupulous deeds of his
earlier career at Medina. Though abating nothing of his
exalted pretentions to be the very Apostle of God,
though claiming for Islam a universal supremacy which
was to brook no opposition and submit to no diminution,
he yet exhibited a calm submission to the will of God
and a perfect reliance on His unmerited mercy for
admission to the Paradise of the Faithful.

MAHOMMED'S BURIAL

THE extraordinary respect and veneration the Mahommedans bore to their Prophet, had been shown by their
anxiety to catch the water used by him in his ablutions
and lick up his spittle and to gather up every hair that
fell from his head or beard preserving the same with
great veneration ; so much the more extreme was the
reverence now paid to his lifeless body. The news of
his death soon spread far and wide throughout Arabia,
and his sorrowing followers hastened in their
thousands from every quarter to obtain a last look

at the venerable face of their Prophet. During the
night the body was washed and laid out in state
for public veneration. His grave was dug on the very
spot where he had breathed his last, and in the evening
of the next day, his red mantle was spread at the bottom
of the grave and the body wrapped in a white sheet of
cloth, was lowered into it; the vault was then covered
in with brickwork and the surface of the grave was
made level with the floor. The tomb is now close to
the great mosque of Medina, which is considered to
rank next to that of Mecca.

MAHOMMED'S PERSON AND CHARACTER

MAHOMMED in person was somewhat above the middle
height, of a handsome and commanding figure. His
head was large and massive with a broad and noble
forehead, thick black hair slightly curling hung over his
ears, his eyebrows arched and joined; his eyes black
and piercing; his nose high and aquiline; a long and
bushy beard rested on his breast; his face had something very winning in its expression and his smile was
gracious and condescending, but when angered his frown
was such, that men quailed before it, and his veins would
swell across his broad forehead when excited. His gait
was quick and decided although he stooped in later
years, and in conversation he was extremly gracious and
turned his full face and whole body towards the speaker.
He treated the most insignificant of his followers with
consideration; visited the meanest and made himself
all to all. He shared in the joys of others, and had a
very sympathetic heart towards those in trouble. He
was gentle and kind to little children. His warm
attachment to Abu Bekr, Ali, Zaid, Othman and Omar
was ardently reciprocated by them. He never assumed
lordly airs, nor demanded personal services; he would

do everything for himself, even mend his own clothes or sandals. He greatly enjoyed food, and was very fond of sweetmeats, honey, cucumbers, and undried dates. He was also very fond of perfumes, as well as the society and charms of women. Ayeshah one of his wives used to say that the Prophet of Allah loved three things most; women, scents and food.

Whatever he may have been in his earlier days, while Kadijah his first wife was alive; in his later years, the attractions and passionate enjoyment of women proved his human frailty more than any other thing, and led to the deplorable abrogation in his own favour of his own laws. An extreme instance of this was, as we have seen, when he longed for the wife of his own adopted son and friend Zaid and producing a revelation from God, took her for his own wife.

Mahommed before his flight to Medina showed some marks of entire sincerity, but to believe that he was self-deceived in every act at Medina, is to stretch self-deception to an extreme. The fact that he produced successive revelations enjoining things he desired to do, may possibly be explained in two ways. Either he deliberately invented the revelations to suit the emergency, or being of an excitable and susceptible nature, his broodings on a subject, induced such a state of intense mental exaltation, that he imagined he heard the appropriate revelation.

His many and cruel executions, his craftiness in planning and allowing assassinations, his treachery in .his attacks on the unarmed during the sacred months, his insatiable hatred towards Jews and Christians, his raids and highway robberies, distinguish him among the most notorious brigands, and make him a tyrant of no mean degree. His unimaginable cruelty as well as the debauchery of his private life, go to show in him a very great degree of moral degeneracy and height of self-delusion, which are scarcely compatible with the practical wisdom of many of his actions.

We find him, after his early struggles and the commencement of his preaching, constantly imbued with fatalistic ideas; he believed in predestination, he had many superstitious beliefs and was guided by omens and prognostications. His many inward struggles, his moral debates, and his aspirations seemed to him the very voice of God speaking to him. Although he pretended to denounce idolatry, and to preach the worship of one true God, still his conduct towards the Kaaba and the superstitious practices he ordained to be practised there, his veneration for the black stone at Kaaba; his superstitious belief in the water of Zem Zem well, all make us doubt whether he really denounced idolatry generally or denounced only such idolatry as did not meet his taste.

However, his denunciation of idolatry on the whole, his preaching the one true God, the equality of man before God, his precepts of charity and fraternal love; his injunctions forbidding the use of liquor and other spirits as well as of the practice of usury to his followers, really distinguish Mahommed honourably as a great religious teacher; though on the other hand his sensuality, deception, cruelty and intolerance stain the Prophet's life to the highest degree and prove him to be both an erring mortal and in no sense an infallible model of conduct.

It is simply astonishing to see over 180 millions of the people of the globe, quite ignorant of the true life and character of the Prophet of Islam, blindly and fanatically profess the religion taught by such a man, fully contented to find that the religion taught by the Prophet besides promising them heavenly paradise after death, gives them full scope in this world to lead a life as easy as one could desire and to satisfy their sensual pleasures to the highest imaginable degree.

THE SUCCESSORS OF MAHOMMED

AFTER the death of Mahommed, it was immediately necessary to choose a successor to the Prophet. A contention arose between the people of Mecca and Medina as to the person who was to succeed Mahommed, because the Prophet had died without leaving male issue. His daughter Fatima was married to his cousin Ali, and therefore Ali laid his claims to be the lawful successor of the Prophet on both these grounds. The dispute however was decided by the influence of Omar in favour of Abu Bekr; because Abu Bekr was the most intimate confidant of the Prophet and was his only companion in the cause before the flight to Medina; and it was Abu Bekr who was chosen by the Prophet to lead the pilgrimage to Mecca as well as to lead the public prayers in the mosque during the Prophet's last illness, as his representative; besides he was the father of Ayesha the favourite wife and the premier of his harem, who herself used all her influence to bring about the election of her father as the successor to the Prophet though her influence was greatly resented by Ali her implacable enemy. The election of Abu Bekr pleased both the people of Mecca and Medina and thus Abu Bekr was saluted as the first Caliph or successor of Mahommed. The dignity of Caliph carried with it the supreme temporal and spiritual authority over the Faithful.

ABU BEKR (632-634 A.D.) gathered together the scattered chapters of the Koran as stated in another chapter. He, after having reduced to submission all those who had contested his authority, bethought himself of the command of Mahommed that 'true Muslims must fight till all people were of the true religion.' He accordingly sent a circular to all the leading men in Arabia, acquainting them with his design and adding that fighting for religion was an act of obedience to God. To engage in the Holy War was the most blessed of all religious duties, and conferred on the combatant a special merit ; and side by side with it lay the bright prospects of spoil and female slaves, conquest and glory. An immense army of greedy and fanatic Muslims gathered around the banner of Abu Bekr. Syria was first attacked, city after city was compelled to open its gates to the all conquering *Saracens*, the name by which the Muslim warriors are known in history. Damascus, the capital of Syria, fell in 634 A.D. before the renowned warrier Khalid, and the relentless soldier made the blood of the Christians stream like water through the streets. On the very day that Damascus was taken, Abu Bekr fell ill, and died a fortnight later.

After the death of Abu Bekr, OMAR (634-643 A.D.) was immediately saluted as the *Commander of the Faithful*, a title which was adopted by the succeeding Caliphs. Under Omar, the Saracen army carried consternation into the adjacent countries. Jerusalem was besieged and its inhabitants were either forced to embrace Islam or to pay heavy tribute. Omar himself travelling on a red camel went in person triumphantly to receive the submission of this glorious capital of the Jews. He caused a magnificent mosque to be erected on the site of the temple of Jerusalem in 637. Meantime Amru one of the generals of Omar brought Egypt under the complete sway of the Caliph. Omar however was not allowed to live long to carry his cruel sword further. Soon after his return to Medina, while engaged at morning prayer in the mosque, he was stabbed to death by a Persian who was enraged at being required to pay tribute. Thus in the very place, from whence his son-in-law the Prophet of Islam had begun to use his sword for the

G

spread of his religion, Omar the father-in-law and second successor of Mahommed fell by the sword.

Omar was the first who bore the title of 'Prince of the Faithful' and though his empire extended from the Orontes to the Arabian Sea and from the Caspian to the Nile, he affected no regal state, was the friend and companion of the beggar and the poor, and was ready to share his meal with the humblest brother in the Faith. Before his death he had confided to six of the chiefs at Medina the selection of a successor and the choice fell on Othman, who had married two of the daughters of the Prophet.

OTHMAN OR USMAN was saluted as Caliph in 644 Following the example of his warlike predecessors, he sought to enlarge his dominions. An army of 40,000 warriors was sent to Africa to subdue it to the faith of Islam ; Cyprus was next conquered and in 651 the kingdoms of the Medes and Persians passed under his rule. The reign of Othman is chiefly remarkable for the revision of the Koran, the text of which was finally fixed. His end however was as tragic as that of his predecessor. While engaged in reading the Koran in his own palace, he was brutally murdered by some of the discontented Arabs in 656 and his corpse was cast into a pit.

Compared with Abu Bekr and Omar simple and zealous apostles of the faith, the character of Othman was in many respects far inferior. Though brave and liberal he was too much inclined to favour his near relatives and personal friends, and this led to great discontentment and ended in his own murder.

ALI, the son-in-law of Mahommed, called the 'Lion of God' whose claims to be the immediate successor of Mahommed had been set aside by the intrigues of Ayshah, was now proclaimed as the successor of Othman in 656. Ali soon raised up many enemies against himself by trying to displace the governors appointed by Othman. The most formidable was Muawiya, governor of Syria, who was afterwards joined by Amru the conqueror of Egypt. Ali was accused before the army, as being guilty of the crime of the murder of Othman. Ayeshah the widow of Mahommed, who had always borne great jealousy and hatred towards Ali, taking advantage of these troubles, raised an army and putting herself at the head of her troops attacked Ali, who however was victorious and Ayeshah herself was taken prisoner. Ali contented himself with bitterly reproaching her for her conduct and, dismissing her courteously, ordered her to spend the remainder of her life at her husband's tomb.

Several bloody battles were fought between the troops of Ali and Muawiya. Three fanatics, to put an end to this disgraceful civil war and to restore peace in Islam, as they thought, conspired to assassinate Muawiya, Amru and Ali. The two first escaped but Ali was assassinated in a mosque at Kufa, after a troublesome reign of little more than five years, in 651.

In the reign of Ali, a division arose among the Mahommedans which still exists. The partisans of Ali consider Abu Bekr, Omar and Othman, as usurpers; and call themselves Shiahs, while the opponents of Ali are called Sunnis.

Hasan, the elder son of Ali was saluted as next Caliph, but he was of a very peaceable disposition and quite ill-fitted to rule such turbulent subjects. He was poisoned by his own wife at the instigation of Muawiya, who afterwards had himself proclaimed as Caliph in succession to Hasan. On the death of Muawiya (679 A.D.) a party at Kufa invited Husain, the younger son of Ali, who had secretly escaped to Mecca, to become Caliph, while a more powerful party favoured Yezid the son of

Muawiya. Husain, contrary to the advice of his friends, set out for Kufa with a small number of followers At Karabala, he was met by a large force, while he had with him only 72 men. After prodigies of valour, Husain fell, his body pierced with 33 wounds. His head was struck off, and was taken to the Governor of Kufa, who struck it over the mouth with a stick. This was on the 10th day of the month of Ramadan or Muharram, in the year 61 of the Hegira, corresponding with 19th October 680 A.D. There is no event in Mahomedan history more mournful than the story of the martyrdom of the sainted Husain. The Shiah sect which pays to Ali and his sons honours not inferior to those given to Mahommed, detests the name of Yezid, and keeps with demonstrations of passionate grief, the festival of Husain's death, and has made his tomb at the Kerbela, a place of pilgrimage hardly inferior to Mecca. The anniversary of his death is religiously observed even to this day, by the erection of the Taboot and by the carrying in procession of the usual standard of the Moslems, the figure of a hand, placed on a pole to represent the full members of the family of the Prophet, namely : Mahommed, his daughter Fatima, her husband Ali and their two sons Hasan and Husain ; and also a spear with a lemon on its point, to represent the head of Husain as it was carried in disgrace to the Governor of Kufa. The martyrdom of the first three Caliphs Ali, Hasan, and Husain of the Shiah sect is commemorated every year on the 10th day of the Muharram.

The decendants of Muawiya, called Ommaides, after Omayya, the famous Korreish leader, from whom Muawiya himself was decended, reigned for fourteen generations from 661 to 750 A.D. During the reign of Muawiya, Damascus was made the capital of the Khalifite Empire. The Ommyads plundered Medina,

took Mecca and even burnt down Kaaba, which, however, was soon rebuilt. They extended their power to
the borders of China, North Africa, and all Spain.
Maewan the last of Omayad Khalifs was slain by a
descendant of Abbas, the paternal uncle of Mahommed.
The descendants of Abbas enjoyed the greatest consideration among the Moslems and on Ali's sons' death,
were the nearest of kin to the prophet. On the fall
of Maewan, Abu al Abbas was saluted as Khalif, the
first of the Abbaside dynasty. Thirty seven Khalifs
of this dynasty reigned over the Mahommedan Empire
from 750 to 1258 A.D. Mansur the second Khalif of
the the Abbaside dynasty removed the seat of the
Empire to Bagdad on the Tigris 762 A.D. In 1258 a
grandson of Genghis Khan the formidible enemy of
the Caliphs took Bagdad and put to death the last
of the Abbasides. Meantime different dynasties arose
side by side each having their own Caliphs. In 910
the Fatimite dynasty was founded in Egypt by Obaid
Allah, surnamed the 'Mahdi' *i.e.* 'the directed one'
that is 'fit to guide others,' and claiming to be a
descendant of Fatimah the daughter of Mahommed.
This dynasty lasted in Egpyt and North Africa till
1171 A.D. Othoman Turks set up their dynasty in
Constantinople in 1299 and it still continues, the
Sultan of Turkey being now usually considered as the
chief Moslim Head, but he is not an Arab and consequently has no claim to the Caliphate.

Thus the empire founded by the camel driver of
Mecca, the prophet of Islam, had from his humble
dwelling at Medina, in no more than a century, extended
throughout Arabia, Syria, and Egypt, along the coast
of Mauritania far into the interior of Africa, and included within its borders, Spain and part of Gaul;
eastward, Persia and Sinai had been subdued and
many other eastern countries had been invaded and

the sovereign will of the 'Commander of the
faithful' gave law from the Indus to the Atlantic.
But this greatness was not to last long. The immense
Empire contained within itself the seeds of its own
dissolution which soon germinated in the ambition of
rival princes and the fury of contending sects. We
uave seen already how one dynasty was supplanted by
another rival dynasty, and how Caliphs were torn to
pieces, causing universal anarchy and ruin. A brave
soldier of the barbarous army, a shrewd bodyguard
of the Caliphs, or a cunning officer of the state, soon
arrogated to themselves the most important offices,
and left to their sovereign only a nominal authority, and
during the height of their usurpation subjected him
to indignity, and even to death.

PART III

THE KORAN

THE Koran (from the Arabic word Quarra, to read) is the sacred book which contains the revelations and doctrines preached by Mahommed, and is held in the highest veneration by his followers. The Koran is not as long as the New Testament and was not reduced to its present form until twenty years after Mahommed's death. The Mahommedans believe that this book was not composed by the Prophet or by any person, but is of divine origin, eternal and co-existing in the very essence of God, written in the so-called 'Preserved Table'; and that a copy of this was sent down from the highest heavens to the lowest heaven in the month of Ramdan on that famous night of power through the ministry of the Angel Gabriel, and that the Angel Gabriel revealed it thence to Mahommed by instalments some at Mecca and some at Medina, at different times during the space of twenty-three years as the exigencies of affairs required, and as it flowed from the inspired lips of the Prophet, it was written down upon palm leaves, leather, etc., by his secretaries Zeid and Abdullah. The amanuenses or secretaries after having distributed the copies to the faithful, many of whom learnt them by heart, placed the originals in a box in no regular order.

We must always bear in mind that Mahommed was no cold systematic thinker, but a real visionary, brought up in the midst of gross superstition and without any proper education. Full of religious dreams and of a highly nervous temperament, he indeed fancied he heard the angel bidding him recite what he imagined to be a revelation, and in uncontrollable excitement his mouth out-poured the supposed revelations, many of which, had they not been immediately taken down in writing by his secretaries, would never have come to light, for the Koran itself admits that the Prophet soon forgot some of his revelations. When Mahommed died, the manuscripts of the revelations were found lying in the box in a diserderly state and Abu Bekr, who on the death of Mahommed, had been chosen by the majority as the first Khalif or successor of Mahommed, ordered Zeid to make a regular collection of the whole of the revelations both of the written ones preserved in the box as well as of such unwritten revelations as could be gathered from the mouths of those who had heard them from the Prophet and had learnt them by heart. When Zeid made the whole collection, Abu Bekr revised them and reduced them to some order, and the whole collection thus revised was given into the custody of Hafsa, one of the widows of Mahommed and daughter of Omar, who had taken great interest in the matter.

In 650 A.D., while Othman was Khalif, a dispute arose regarding the true text of the Koran, and Othman gave orders to Zeid to make a fresh revision of the text with the help of three other divines and all the previous copies of the Koran were called in and were destroyed. This recension of Zeid has been so carefully preserved from that time to this day, quite unaltered, that there is but one and the same Koran in use throughout the vast bounds of the Mahommedan world. Variations in the text are almost unknown. There is every probability that the work of Zeid was executed faithfully, and indeed, the acceptance of the Koran by Ali and his party, the antagonists of the unfortunate Othman, is the surest guarantee of its genuineness. It is possible that some of the earlier and more ephemeral fragments which proceeded from Mahommed may before his death have become obsolete, and thus escaped notice ; but the pious veneration with which the whole body of the Mussulmans from the very first regarded his revelations as the word of God, the devotion with which they committed them to memory, and the evidence that transcripts existed even from an early period of Mahommed's ministry, combined with the fact that Zeid's collection came into immediate and unquestionable use all leave no doubt in the mind that the Koran contains the very words delivered by the Prophet. The few variations are confined almost entirely to the vowel forms, and the diacritical points are the inventions of a latter period, which were not existent in Zeid's original. In a work extending over so many years, based upon the changing incidents of the day, and bearing so manifestly the impress of an impulsive mind, discrepancies were to be expected, and they certainly are not wanting in the Koran. Another thing deserves remark here : while some of the smaller suras or chapters are more or less complete, and presumably in the form in which they were first promulgated, there prevails throughout the great body of the work, an utter disregard of chronological sequence. There are not only startling breaks and gaps, but latter passages not unfrequently precede the earlier. When the component parts of each sura are thus often wanting in connection, whether of time or subject, the several suras or chapters follow one another upon no principle whatever, excepting it be that of length.

The Koran is written with the utmost elegance and purity of language in the dialect of the tribe of Koreish the most noble and polite of all the Arabian dialects. It is written in rhythmic prose the jingling sounds of which greatly delight the Arabs. The Mussulmans believe that the style of the Koran in elegance and in composition is such that it is inimitable by human pen and therefore the composition of the Koran itself is a miracle.

The general design of the Koran seems to unite into one religion the people of the three different religions then prevalent in Arabia, namely the idolators, the Jews and the Christians.

The Koran is divided into one hundred and fourteen chapters or Suras, containing in all about six thousand two hundred verses. It is arranged in thirty sections called Juz or Siparch to enable a Moslem to recite the whole in the space of thirty days of Ramadan. The chapters are generally titled from some leading word occurring in each, *v.g.*, cow, woman, table, etc.

Such is the veneration paid to the Koran that no Moslem would dare to touch it without first being purified with water, and they read it with the greatest care and respect. They swear by it, consult it on all occasions, carry it with them to war, write sentences from it on their banners, house-doors or walls, or on copper plates which they suspend from their necks as charms, and many try to learn by heart as much of it as possible. A man who is able to repeat the whole Koran by heart is called a Hafig or protector, though he may not understand a word of it.

THOUGH the Koran is the ground-work and essential standard of Moslem orthodoxy and its authority is quite absolute in all matters of polity, ethics and science equally as in matters of religion and to it every reference is primarily made; yet as Islam extended its borders and took the shape of a vast empire, to regulate its social and political relations as well as for the administration of justice in evil and criminal cases, some more extended and discriminating code became necessary. This deficiency was supplied by the compilation of the 'Sunnah' or 'Traditional Law' which is built upon the sayings and practices of Mahommed, and in the opinion of the orthodox is invested with the force of law and of the authority of inspiration, because it is the belief among the Moslems that their prophet, in all things that he did and all that he said, was guided by God, and his words and actions are therefore to be for ever a divine rule of faith and practice. Hence these traditions are regarded by Moslems as a great canonical authority, and next to the Koran the most sacred book of Moslem faith. The collections of these traditions are also called 'Hadis.'

The traditions appear to have remained unwritten for about a century after the death of Mahommed, when they were partly collected by Omar II, and the work was continued by his successors. An incredible number of so-called 'Traditions' fabricated for the purpose of upholding certain political and sectarian claims, were subsequently rejected and the Sunnah were condemned and promulgated for the guidance of the faithful. The six standard Sunni collections were compiled exclusively under the Abbaside Caliphs about the years 814-834 A.D. The four canonical collections of the Shiahs were pre-

pared somewhat later, and are much less trustworthy
than the former, because their chief object was to build
up the divine headship of Ali and his descendants.
Though these two sects, Sunnis and Shiahs, are considered sound in fundamentals, they differ in some
points of law and religion, and while the former adhere
scrupulously to the Sunnahs, the latter adhere to their
own traditions and reject the authority of the ' Sunnah,'
and assert that the sovereign or Imamat or temporal and
spiritual headship over the faithful was by divine right
vested in Ali and in his descendants through Hasan
and Hosein the children of Fatima, the daughter of the
prophet, and they add to the formula of belief, the
confession ' Ali is the Caliph of God.'

IMAN OR THE CREED OF ISLAM

IT may be as well here to enter somewhat more fully
into the meaning of some of the principal terms we
have been using in this book. Iman signifies the
doctrine of Islam and Kalima is a word denoting the
brief Summary of the doctrine of Islam ; Islam means
submission and is used to denote the religion of
Mahommed, signifying submission to the service and
command of God. Those who profess the religion of
Islam are also called Muslims or Moslems, Mussulmans,
being the Persian form of the original Arabic word for
Islam. Imams are leaders in prayer and they are the
important officials of the mosques, in other words they
are the clergy of the Moslems ; the chief Caliphs are
also sometimes called Immams. Qazi is the chief
Judge who passes sentences in all cases, Mufti is the
official referee who supplies decrees (fetwa) to the Judge
in difficult cases, based on the Koran or the rulings of
the great orthodox doctors ; Moulvies or Moullas are
learned doctors and teachers of religion. The word

Sheikh, corresponding to Presbyter or elder, is a title of respect; and Sultan is the highest authority in matters of civil and ecclesiastical affairs.

The Mahommedans divide their religion (Islam) into two distinct parts; *Iman i.e.*, Faith or Theory and *Din i.e.*, religion or practice and the whole of Islam is built on five fundamental points, of which one belongs to Iman or faith and the four others appertain to Din or practice. The whole creed or Imam is divided into six Kalimas or articles, namely (1) Belief in God, (2) Belief in his Angels, (3) Belief in his scriptures, (4) Belief in his prophets, (5) Belief in the resurrection and in the day of Judgment, (6) Belief in God's absolute decrees and predetermination both of good and evil. In brief it may be summed up in the short act of the profession of Faith, viz : ' I believe in God, Angels, Books, Prophets, the last day, the predestination by God of the good and evil and the resurrection of the dead.' The four points relating to Din or practice are, (1) Prayer, (2) Alms, (3) Fasting, (4) Pilgrimage to Mecca.

The Koran opens with the famous chapter of prayer which Muslims regard as the essence of the Koran and repeat as Christians do the Lord's Prayer; besides it is the model of the rhyme and of the jingling sounds which so greatly delight the Moslems. As an example I shall quote this much venerated chapter called in Arabic Al-Fatchat :

Bismillá-hi'rahmáni'rrahím.
Al-hamdúlilláhi Rabbi' lálumin.
Arrahmáni'rrahim ;
Máliki yomi-d-din.
Iyáka Nábúdú, waiyáka nastáín.
Ihdina'ssirát al mústakím ;
Sirát alazina an niámta alaihim,
Ghairi-'l-mághdhúbi alaihim waladhálína.

' In the name of God, the Compassionate, the Merciful.
Praise be to God, Lord of all the worlds !
The Compassionate, the Merciful !
King on the Day of Judgment !
Thee do we worship, and to Thee do we cry for help !
Guide Thou us on the right path !
The path of those to whom Thou art gracious !
Not of those with whom Thou art angered, nor of those
    who go astray.'

THE EXPLANATION OF THE ARTICLES OF FAITH

THE Imam or creed as we have seen above is divided
into six articles.

I. *Belief in God* : The unity of God is declared in
Sura 112. Mahommed and his followers in general
seem to have had a fairly correct idea of God, and more
or less of his attributes. Of course they most obstin-
ately reject the mystery of the Blessed Trinity, which
is a great stumbling block to Muslims whose religion
knows or admits no mysteries. The Koran teaches
that God is eternal, everlasting, indivisible, not endued
with form, not circumscribed by limit or measure, com-
prehending all things but comprehended of nothing,
and that he has ninety-nine different names expressing
most of his attributes. The Muslims make use of
beads (Rosary) to repeat these ninety-nine different
names of God because Mahommed has promised those
of his followers who recited these ninety-nine names
of God devoutly, a sure entrance into Paradise. The
Wahabees, however, rejecting the use of beads or
rosary, count these names on their fingers. Their idea
of God so far is not much different from that held by
Jews and Christians. In Sura 6 it is stated that God has
no offspring, because He has no consort, God is also
represented as creating both evil and good. In Sura 2

God is said to have taught Adam, whom He had created
from earth, the names of all things, and to have ordered
angels to worship Adam and that all angels did worship
Adam, as they were ordered except the angel Eblis, who,
therefore, was converted into Satan.

II. *Belief in Angels.* The Koran represents God as
attended by Angels or pure beings created from fire,
who act according to God's order, and who do not rebel
against Him. They neither eat nor drink, nor propagate their species, having no sex ; some of them are
employed to be near God, to sing his praises, or to
intercede for mankind, while some others act as God's
messengers, or write down the actions of man. Two
angels are assigned to each man standing the one at his
right called Rhazwan and the other called Malik
at his left side ; both record all the actions of a
man. The Koran makes mention of four chief Angels :
Gabriel whose chief duty is to communicate God's will
to prophets ; Michael the friend and protector of the
Jews and guardian of rain, grain and of all that
is required for the support of man, beasts, and fishes ;
Israfel whose office is to sound the last trumpet on the
day of ressurrection ; and Azrael the angel of death who
separates men's souls from their bodies. The Muslims
are also taught to believe in two fierce looking black
Angels, Munkir and Nakir, who are charged by God
to visit every man in his grave, and to examine him with
regard to his faith in God and in Mahommed.
Mahommed seems to have entirely borrowed the whole
doctrine concerning angels from Jews and Persians.
The ancient Persians believed in the ministry of angels
and their supervision over the affairs of this world.
The Jews likewise believed that the angels were created
of fire and that they hold several offices, and that they
intercede for man. They too believed in the Angel
of Death whom they called ' Duma ' and that he called

each man by his name at the death bed. The devil as known in the Koran as Eblis or Shaitan is plainly adopted from Jewish and Christian sources. Mahommed taught that devils or Eblis were once of the number of those who stood near God, but because they refused to obey God by doing homage to Adam, they were thrust out of heaven. Besides angels and devils, the Koran teaches belief in the existence of Jin or Genii, created also of fire, but of a grosser fabric than of angels and these eat, drink, and propagate their species and are subject to death. It is supposed that some of these are good and others evil, and that they are capable of meriting salvation or damnation. It is said that they were created several ages before Adam and were under the government of several successive princes, who all bore the common name of Soloman ; but at length they fell into general corruption, and Eblis was sent to drive them into a remote part of the earth beyond the known world and there they are kept confined.

III. *Belief in Books.* The Mahommedans are taught in the Koran that God in diverse ages of the world, sent down from heaven his revelations in writing to several prophets. The total number of Books thus sent number 104 ; of which 10 were given to Adam, 50 to Seth ; 30 to Enoch or Edris ; 10 to Abraham and the remaining four, the Taurat (Pentateuch) was sent to Moses. The Zabur (Psalms) was delivered to David. The Ingil (The Gospels) was revealed to Jesus and the Koran was made known to Mahommed, who, being the last and greatest of the prophets, these revelations are now closed and no more are to be expected. All these divine books except the last four, the Mahommedans say, are now lost and their contents are unknown, and of the four existing books, the first three have been corrupted by Jews and Christians and hence no credit whatever is to be given to them. The Moslems however have never said at what period, or by whom, or in what manner these books have been corrupted. The Mahommedans pretend also to posssess a book (forged and apochryphal) called 'the Barnabas' Gospel,' which they claim to have been written by the apostle Barnabas, wherein the history of Jesus Christ is related in a manner very different from that mentioned in the other Gospels, and which to a very great degree corresponds to traditions which Mahommed has related in the Koran. This book does not appear to have been originally a forgery of the Mahommedans, though they have no doubt interpolated and altered it since, the better to serve their purpose, and in particular instead of the Paraclete or Comforter as in John xiv. 16-26, they have in this apocryphal gospel inserted the word ' Periclyte,' that is, 'the famous ' or 'the illustrious ' which they pretend proves that their prophet was foretold by Jesus Christ (Nominatim) by name, that being the signification of Mahommed in Arabic.

IV. *Belief in Prophets* : The number of Prophets, who have been sent by God into the world to instruct men from time to time according to the doctrine taught by Mahommed, amounts to 224,000, among whom 313 were apostles who were sent with a special mission to reclaim mankind from infidelity and superstition. Six of these are the most distinguished who brought down new laws, successively abrogating the preceding ones ; they are : Adam, Noah, Abraham, Moses, Jesus and Mahommed, the last is said to be the greatest and the seal of the Prophets, since after him no other prophet is to be expected. All these six prophets are said to have received from God inspired books, but they are all superseded by the Koran. All the prophets in general, the Mahommedans believe to have been free from great sins, and errors of consequence and to have

G

been professors of one and the same religion, that is Islam, notwithstanding the different laws and institutions which they observed. They allow degrees among them and hold some of them to be more excellent and honourable than others. (Koran, Sura II.) As Mahommed acknowledged the divine authority of the Pentateuch, Psalms, and Gospels, he often appealed to the consonancy of the Koran with those writings ; and to the prophecies which he pretended were contained therein concerning himself, as proofs of his mission and he frequently charged the Jews and the Christians with suppressing the passages which bear witness to him ; forgetting that those writings were centuries older than the Prophet, and that before he came into the world, they had been in the hands of Jews and Christians for several hundred years.

The Resurrection and the Day of Judgment. Mahommedans teach that when a corpse is laid down in the grave, an angel gives him notice of the coming of the two black angels, Munkir and Nakir, to examine his deeds. They make the dead person sit upright, and his soul then re-enters the body, and if his faith in God and in Mahommed answers rightly to the questions put to him, he is refreshed with the air of paradise ; otherwise his corpse is pressed hard to the ground and he is beaten with iron rods and his corpse is kept there stung till the day of resurrection by ninety-nine dragons. These most ridiculous and absurd notions, especially when we consider that many people are burnt or devoured by wild beasts, seem to have been borrowed by Mahommed and his followers from the early Jews, among whom some similar notions prevailed. The Mahommedans believe that the souls of the departed are not admitted into heaven immediately after death, but will have to wait till the day of resurrection, unless one had the privilege of being a prophet. They say that the souls are allowed to remain near the sepulchre with liberty to go wherever they please. The souls of the wicked, however, are confined in a filthy dungeon, where they are tormented. The Mahommedans profess that the time of resurrection is a secret known to God alone and this secret has not been communicated even to the angel Gabriel or to Mahommed ; however, they say that the approach of that terrible day may be known from certain signs which will precede it, such as universal decay of faith, tumults and seditions everywhere, the rising of the sun in the West, the appearance of a monstrous beast sixty cubits high, the personal presence of an antichrist with one eye and marked on the forehead with the letters C.F.R. signifying Cafer or infidel, the descent of Jesus on earth, who would then embrace the faith of Mahommed, take a wife and beget children, and then kill the antichrist and restore peace to the world and after a peaceful reign of forty years, would die. During the reign of Jesus, they say there will be great security, and plenty in the world, all malice and hatred being laid aside ; lions, camels, bears and sheep shall live in peace and a child shall play with serpents unhurt. Then a dark smoke shall fill the whole earth ; the Kaaba will be demolished ; this will be followed by the coming of Mahdi or Director out of the family of Mahommed and whose name as Mahommed prophesied, should be as his own name, and whose father's name should also be the same as his own father's name and who shall govern all the Arabians in his name, and who shall again fill the earth with righteousness, and at last the Angel Israfel shall blow the first sound of his trumpet, known as the blast of consternation, at which the whole earth will tremble, the heavens will melt away, the sun, the moon, and the stars shall be thrown into the sea which will turn into flames. This

will be followed by the sounding of the second blast
called the blast of extermination, when all the creatures
both in heaven and on earth shall die or be annihilated.
Forty years after the second blast, the third blast, called
the blast of resurrection will be blown, God meantime
having raised to life the angels Israfel, Gabriel and
Michael, and after the third blast is blown by the
resuscitated Angel Israfel, all these three angels shall
stand up on the rock of the temple of Jerusalem and
shall call all the dead to life again, and to appear before
the judgment seat ; at which all the souls shall run to
their respective bodies, which the earth opening its
mouth, shall allow to rise. The first to rise will be
Mahommed himself, and then all the rest shall spring
from their graves as soon as the signal is given by
the last sound of the trumpet of Israfel, all barefooted,
naked and uncircumcised, just as they came out of their
mother's womb. Further the Mahommedans believe
that those who are destined to be partakers of eternal
happiness will rise in honour and security, and those
who are doomed to misery, in disgrace and in dismay,
and that all will be assembled divided into three
different classes, the first to consist of those believers
whose good works have been few, and these will
go on foot ; the second to consist of those who have
led a pious life and have been in greater honour with
God, and these shall ride on white winged camels with
saddles of gold, and the third composed of wicked
sinners and infidels and these shall appear with ten
different distinguishing marks : (1) the ungodly in the
form of apes, (2) the public oppressors like swine, (3)
the usurers with reversed heads and distorted feet, (4)
the unjust judges will appear blind, (5) the vain-
glorious will be deaf and dumb, (6) the hypocrites will
gnaw their tongues which will hang down all bleeding,
(7) the defrauders with hands and feet cut off, (8)

the false accusers and culumniators, fixed to the trunks
of palm trees, (9) the voluptuous and the miserly with
stinking corpses, and (10) the proud and arrogant
with clothes daubed with pitch.

As to the length of time the judgment will take the
Koran says one thousand years, but the place where
this judgment will take place, is not known. The
Koran itself is quite silent on this point. Further the
Mahommedans believe that on the last day not only
men shall be judged but also irrational animals and
genii.

The Judgment. Men will be raised again to life and
they will render an account of all their actions, after
which they will receive their reward. As soon as they
are raised to life, all men both just and wicked shall
be filed by the angels into ranks according to their
actions and then with great anxiety and fear, they will
remain waiting the judgment. Then God shall appear
to judge all men, Mahommed undertaking the office
of intercessor, after it shall have been declined by Adam,
Moses and Jesus, who will pray for the deliverance
of their own souls. Then God surrounded by his
angels will sit in judgment, the guardian angels producing books wherein are recorded all the actions of each
man ; after which every one will be permitted to make
his own defence, during which disputes will rise even
between body and soul, the one accusing and blaming
the other. Then they will be weighed in a big balance
of two scales held by angel Gabriel in his hand, one of
which will hang over paradise and the other over
hell. God will then give to every one his dues, the
righteous shall be sent to dwell among delights, and
the unjust and wicked ones shall be thrust into hell
fire. Those who are to be admitted into paradise
shall stand on the right, and the wicked on the left, and
both shall be made to pass over a bridge called ' Al-Sirat '

thinner than the hair and sharper than the edge of a
sword, hanging over the abyss of hell. The good ones
led by Mahommed shall pass over the bridge with
wonderful ease and alacrity, while the wicked will soon
miss their footing and fall down headlong into the abyss
of hell, which shall be gaping beneath them. According
to Mahommedans, hell is divided into seven regions
destined to receive the different classes of the damned.
The first region is called 'Jehennam' where the wicked
Mahommedans will be tormented for a time, until they
are released and taken up into heaven. The second
region is called Ladha for Jews, the third one called
Hotama destined for Christians, fourth, Al-Sair for
the Sabians, fifth Sakar for the Magians, sixth al-Jehim
for the idolators, and the seventh and last which is the
lowest and worst of all called Al Hawiyat is for the
hypocrites, or those who outwardly professed some
religion, but in their hearts were of none. Both
in the Koran and Traditions various kinds of torments
by which the damned are tormented in hell, are minutely
described, such as excessive cold or intense heat, and
the severity of their pains in hell shall be in proportion
to their crimes. The greatest pain of the infidel shall
be their despair that they must remain there for ever ;
for the Moslems cast into hell shall be delivered from
hell-fire after a time, and their burnt skin having
been revived by being washed with the *water of life,*
they will be received into heaven.

Heaven is thus described. The Mahommedans are
taught to believe that the righteous after crossing the
sharp bridge, shall be refreshed by drinking of the
famous Mahommed's pond, whose water is whiter than
milk and more fragrant than musk. This is the first
taste the blessed shall have of their future and ap-
proaching felicity. Paradise is situated in the seventh
heaven next under the throne of God, its floor is laid with

finest wheat flour, its stones are pearls, the walls of the
buildings within are of gold and silver, and the trees
of paradise are of gold, among which is the most famous
tree called 'Tuba' or the tree of happiness, the branches
of which will reach to the apartments of every blessed
and will be laden with exquisite fruits and other eatables,
the taste of which is unknown to mortals and the
peculiarity of this tree will be such that it will produce
any fruit or any thing whatsoever that the blessed
in paradise may desire to possess. The whole of
paradise is supplied by three rivers, one flowing with
water, the second flowing with milk, and the third with
wine and honey. Each blessed one will be supplied
with mansions furnished with the richest furniture, the
floor will be covered with silken carpets, the couches,
litters, nay even pillows and beds will not only be very
fine and soft but will be embroidered with gold and
precious stones. But all these glories and pleasures
will be eclipsed by the resplendent and ravishing girls
of paradise, the enjoyment of whose company will be
the principal happiness of the faithful. The damsels
of paradise are not made of clay as mortal women, but
of pure musk and are free from natural impurities and
defects, and live under pavilions of hollow pearls.
Mahommedans call this happy mansion, the garden
of paradise 'Jannat al Ferdaws' or the garden of
pleasures, 'Jannat al Naim' and the like. Further they
assert that the blessed will be welcomed into paradise
by beautiful youths, who are destined to be their pages,
and then each one will be clothed with the garments of
paradise and rings of exceeding beauty will be placed
on his fingers; each will be further provided with
seventy-two damsels of paradise for wives together with
all or any of the wives he had in the world. God will
send him also presents of loaves of bread of the most
delicious taste, and for meat he will have the flesh of

the fat ox called Balan and the fish Nun. In this manner the blessed ones will be welcomed and entertained on their admission into paradise, after which each one will be sent to the mansion assigned him, the beauty and felicity of which will be proportioned to his merits, but far beyond anyone's expectation or comprehension. There they will be served in vessels of gold with foods of most delicious taste, wines of exquisite flavour ; and time will pass in endless pleasure and delight with the houris of paradise. The whole heavens will resound with the ravishing songs of angels, and all the mansions will be perfumed with sweet and delightful fragrance.

It is not difficult to show that Mahommed borrowed many of his ideas of the happiness of paradise from Jews among whom had prevailed the idea that the mansions of the just in heaven were like a delicious garden with three gates, and having four rivers flowing with milk, honey, wine and balsam. It is not improbable that he also received some ideas of the felicity of the just in the next life from the Christians, who often described in figurative language the happiness of heaven. Even in holy Scripture we find celestial enjoyments represented in a figurative manner by means of corporeal objects, and the mansions of the blessed in heaven described as a glorious and magnificent city built of gold and precious stones with twelve gates, through the streets of which runs the river of the water of life ; and our Lord Jesus Christ himself speaks of the future state of the blessed as a kingdom where they shall eat and drink at His table. But these metaphorical images have none of the puerile imaginings which make up the heaven depicted by Mahommed, much less any distant shadow of those sensual allurements held out by Mahommed who, to enhance the value of paradise in the minds of the Arabians, chose to imitate the indecency of the

Magians. Had Mahommed informed his followers that
what he had told them about the pleasures of paradise
should be understood not literally but in a metaphorical
sense, this perhaps would have made some atonement,
but the contrary is so evident from the whole tenor of
the Koran that while a few refined and more enlightened
Mahommedans contend that the description should be
taken in an allegorical or spiritual sense ; yet the
orthodox Moslems in general declare the whole should
be accepted and believed strictly in the obvious and
literal sense. It is an error to say that Mahommedans
hold that women have no souls, or if they have, they
will perish like those of brute beasts and will not be
rewarded in the next life. There are several passages
in the Koran which affirm that women in the next
life, will not only be punished for their evil actions,
but will also receive the reward of their good deeds as
well as the men and that in this case God will make
no distinction of sexes. It is true they will not be
admitted into the same mansion as the men are, because
their places will be supplied by the houris, together
with such of a man's former wives, as he may now also
desire to have. But the good women will go into a
separate place of happiness where they will enjoy all
sorts of delights.

Predestination of good and evil. The sixth great
point of faith which the Muslims are taught by the
Koran, is to believe in God's absolute decrees and the
predestination both of good and evil. The doctrine
is that everything that happens in the world whether
it be good or evil, proceeds entirely from God's will
which is irrevocably fixed and recorded from all eternity
in the so-called preserved table. God has predetermined in the most minute parttcular not only the adverse
or prosperous fortunes of every man, but also his faith
or infidelity ; obedience or disobedience ; his happiness

or misery in this life as well as in the next; and it is
not possible for man by any foresight or wisdom to
avoid what has been thus predetermined by God. The
prophet of Islam made great use of this doctrine in his
Koran for the advancement of his designs and especially
when he met with any adversities or reverses in war.
It is true there are some passages in the Koran which
attribute free will to man and consequent responsi-
billty for his actions, but on the other hand there
are many other passages which clearly and distinctly
teach fatalism, which make God the author of evil and
teach that God decrees man to sin and go to hell; and
as said above, in the advancement of his designs the
prophet made great use of this doctrine to encourage
his followers to fight without fear, and even desperately,
for the propagation of their faith, by representing to
them that all their caution could not avert their
inevitable destiny or prolong their lives for a moment.
This doctrine of absolute election and reprobation so
derogatory to the goodness and justice of God has been
softened down by many thoughtful Mahommedans by
many subtle distinctions, and hence we have several
sects which hold different opinions on this subject.

THE DUTIES OF ISLAM (DIN)

WE have examined briefly the six different articles of
the Imam or Faith of the Moslems as it is taught in the
Koran and Traditions; we shall now examine the teaching of the same books regarding Din or practices of
Islam. We have already mentioned that the fundamental
points relating to Din or practices of Islam are four
viz., Prayer, Ahm, Fasting, and Pilgrimage to Mecca.
We shall see what is taught on each of these fundamental points.

The Koran enjoins on all Muslims the devout recital

of Kaliama or Moslem creed, and the Namaz or prayers including the legal washings or purifications which are considered as necessary preparations for the prayers. The Mahommedans are enjoined to recite daily at least the short form of Kalima or creed, namely 'I testify that there is no God but God and that Mahommed is the Apostle of God.'

Mahommed called prayer the pillar of religion and the key of paradise, and that this important duty of Prayer might not be neglected by his followers, he ordered them to pray five times in every twenty-four hours, at certain fixed times, namely: (1) in the morning at dawn before sun rise; (2) when noon is past; that is just after mid-day; (3) In the afternoon, that is mid time between noon and sunset; (4) In the evening immediately after sunset; (5) At night, mid-time between sunset and mid-night. Mahommed stated that he received this command from the throne of God Himself, when he was carried to heaven in that famous night journey. He, moreover, enjoined that at the time for prayer the Muedhins or Muzzins (that is criers) should ascend the steeple of the mosques and give 'Azan' (*i.e.*, call for prayer), public notice of the time of prayer, as Mahommedans do not make use of bells as Christians do for similar purposes, and at the cry of the Muzzin all Mussulmans should prepare themselves for prayer.

The first important preparation before prayer is the legal washing or ablution, which is an essential duty. The Koran in Sura v says, 'O believers, when you prepare yourself to prayer, wash your faces and hands up to the elbows and rub your heads and your feet up to the ankles.' The Koran enjoins two kinds of purifications: Ghuslor the ablution of the whole body, which is to be invariably made after certain kinds of defilements, and Wazu, the washing of the face, hands, head, and feet after a certain manner, such as rinsing the mouth three times ; putting the water into the nostrils three times, and while performing these purifications short prayers are recited. This ablution called Wazu must be done by every person before he can enter upon the duty of prayer. Lest so necessary a preparation before prayer should be omitted under any pretext, Mahommed ordered that where water cannot be had, or where the use of water becomes prejudicial to one's health, fine clean sand may be used instead. Thus one can see how the most trivial ceremonial observances have been raised into duties of the greatest importance, and as the virtue of prayer is made to depend practically on ablution, ablution is useless unless done in the order prescribed ; so much so that if a man were to wash his left hand before his right hand, or his nose before his teeth, his prayer becomes useless, nay he cannot lawfully say his Namaz, which is all well calculated to make men simple formalists and nothing more.

After performing these prescribed purifications, and after the Muzzin gives the call for prayer in these words, *God is great. I testify there is no God but God, and that Mahommed is his apostle, prayer is betteer than sleep, come to prayers, come to salvation,* the Moslem worshipper should go either to the Mosque or to a place entirely free from impurity. The prayers are said in Arabic, and it is not necessary that the worshipper should understand the words of the prayer. The Traditions further prescribe that when one says his prayers, he must have something in front of him, but if he cannot find anything, he should at least spread a cloth before him or put his walking stick into the ground in front of him, and if the ground be so hard as not to allow this, then the stick should be placed length ways before him ; but if he has neither a cloth to spread or a walking stick to place before him, he must at least draw a line by hand on the ground in front of him, and his attention should not travel beyond this boundary line, and any one passing in front of him beyond this line will not vitiate his prayers. This is the reason why in Mosques the places on which the faithful say their prayers are marked by a boundry line in the form of an oblong figure. During prayer a deep concentrated attention of mind and body is enjoined so that any travelling of the eyes or mind beyond the boundary line, or even a cough suffices to vitiate the prayer, and the worshipper must recite all the prayers over again. While praying Mahommedans are required to turn their faces towards the temple of Mecca. They must also be dressed decently but not sumptuously and therefore they are to lay aside any costly raiment or rich ornaments lest they should seem proud when they approach the Divine presence. They moreover must not admit their women to pray with them in public, because the presence of women is apt to inspire a different kind of devotion from that which is requisite while praying, or while one is in the place dedicated to the worship of God ; therefore, women must perform their prayers apart, whether they pray in their own houses or come to the Mosque for the prayers. Women are not allowed in the Mosque when men are engaged there in prayers, and should they come at such times they must go to a part quite separate from where the men are praying.

The Moslem worshipper having thus composed himself for prayer, observing scrupulously every formality of the preparation, commences what is called the Namaz or prayer during the course of which various picturesque ceremonies are observed. He first stands straight with the hands hanging on either side and says, *I have purposed to offer up to God only with a sincere heart, with my face turned towards the Kibla* (Kaaba).

Then, with the thumbs touching the ears and hands
open on each side of the face, he says, *God is Great*.
After which placing his right hand upon his left hand
just below the navel he repeats, *Holiness to Thee, O God!
And Praise be to Thee! Great is Thy Name! Great
is Thy Greatness, There is no deity but Thee. I seek
refuge near God, from cursed Satan*; *In the name of
God the Compassionate, the Merciful*. Then follows
the recital of the Al-Fatihat, the first chapter of the
Koran (the Mahommedan 'Our Father'), and also
some other chapters of the Koran, repeated by heart;
at the conclusion bending forward with his hands placed
upon his knees, the fingers separated a little, he repeats;
*God is Great! I extol the holiness of my Lord the
Great* (thrice); and then standing upright with the
hands placed on either side, *God hears him who
praises Him*; *O Lord Thou art praised*; then dropping
on his knees he says *God is Great*, and then prostrate
and touching the ground with his nose first and then
with his forehead, he repeats three times, *I extol |the
holiness of my Lord the most High*, making the prostrations with each repetition of the prayer. Then raising
his head and body, he sits backwards upon his heels
and placing his hands upon his thighs, says, *I rise and
sit by the power of God*, and then makes again the
three prostrations as before, repeating the same prayer
each time, *God is Great, I extol the holiness of my Lord
the most High*; he then stands up straight and again
touching the ears with his thumbs and with hands open
repeats the same prayer, *God is Great, I seek forgiveness from God my Lord and I repent before Him*, and
this is followed by the concluding part called the
'Salam' which is done by sitting backwards on the
heels as stated above, placing the hands on the thighs,
and turning the head first to the right and then to the
left each time repeating the concluding prayer, *The*

peace and mercy of God be with you, and thus the Namaz is concluded.

The prayers are shortened or lengthened according to the zeal and the piety of the worshipper, the pious often reciting several chapters of the Koran during these prayers.

Again it is to be remarked that not only is the virtue of prayer made dependent entirely upon trivial ceremonial observances, but even the prescription of such minute and intricate ceremonials and bodily postures during the very course of the prayers with no kind of relevancy to the context of the prayer is apt to keep the mind more concentrated on the right observance of these minute ceremonies than on the meaning of the prayer. When we consider that the prayers of the Namaz are to be said only in the Arabic language, though the worshipper may not understand a word of it, and that it is not necessary that the worshipper should understand even the sense of the prayer he is required to say. the actual prayer which Mahommed calls the pillar of religion and the key of paradise becomes no more than a pure mechanical exercise, a mere parrot cry.

Pious Mahommedans generally are so punctual in the recital of their prayers at the stated times of the day, that not unfrequently, quite unmindful of their surroundings, without the least hesitation or backwardness, they start their prayers and their deep attention and very serious performance of the various picturesque rituals notwithstanding any surrounding distractions, become on the whole a subject for real admiration, if not for edification.

Public services are held on Fridays, when long prayers are repeated, and several chapters of the Koran read, and Khutbas or sermons are usually preached. There are also special prayers for extraordinary occasions such as drought, war, pestilence, and at a funeral.

These purifications, the numerous daily prayers, the different postures and prostrations to testify the solemn act of adoration of God, the turning of the face towards Kibla, were all no doubt borrowed by Mahommed from the Jews as they correspond to a large extent with those in vogue among them. For Jews as well as Arabians, even long before the advent of Mahommed, had similiar ablutions before prayers and meals. The Jews were accustomed to use various postures and prostrations during prayers, which they were enjoined to say three three times a day, turning their faces towards Jerusalem, wearing on their bodies clean garments, men and women praying in separate places apart from each other. All these Jewish practices the prophet of Islam enjoined on his followers.

The second fundamental precept of Din is the giving of *Alms*. Mahommed names two classes of alms, namely Zacat or legal alms and Sadakat or voluntary alms. The zacat or legal alms are of indispensible obligation, being commanded by the law which directs and determines both the kind and the proportion to be given by every Muslim of full age annually on account of his property, provided he has sufficient means for his subsistence and possesses an income equal to about fifty Rupees a year. The rate varies, generally one fortieth part of one's income is considered the legal moiety to be given in alms. This rate or proportion increases for incomes from cattle or lands that are watered by natural sources, in which case one tenth is the legal portion. The Sadakat or voluntary alms are those offered willingly by pious people, who are highly extolled in the Koran. The giving of arms combined with prayer is strongly recommended in the Koran, and the Traditions say that Prayer carries us half-way to God, fasting brings us to the door of His palace and alms-deeds procure for us admission into heaven. The Mahommedans therefore esteem alms-deeds to be highly meritorious and many of them have been famous for the exercise thereof; and the generality are so addicted to the doing of good to others, that they even extend their charities to brute animals. Here again we see traces of Mahommed's indebtedness to the Jews who were conspicuous for their charity, and whose custom it was to give a portion of their income and of their harvest in charity for the poor.

The third great point of Din prescribed by the Koran is *fasting*; a duty of such great importance that Mahommed used to call it 'the gate of heaven.' According to Mahommedan divines there are three kinds of fasts: (1) The restraint of the stomach and other parts of the body from the pleasures of lust and other appetites; (2) The restraint of one's ears, eyes, tongue, hands, feet, and other members of the body from unlawful deeds; (3) The fasting of the heart from worldly cares, and the refraining of the mind from worldly thoughts. Mahommedans are obliged to fast the whole month of Ramadan, that is from the time the new moon in that month first appears till the next appearance of the new moon, during which time they must abstain from eating, drinking, and all pleasures from day break to sunset; after sunset till next day break, however, they are allowed every kind of enjoyment. The Mussulmans observe this fast so strictly that during it they suffer nothing to enter into their mouths, not even would they swallow their own spittle intentionally or even take a bath. Travellers and sick persons are exempted from this fast, but they are obliged to make up for it on some other days when they will be free from any impediment. Like-wise children, old persons and women with suckling babes, are exempted from the fasts.

I

From the earliest days Ramadan (the ninth month of the Mahommedan year) had been held in very great esteem by Arabs, even long before Mahommed's time, and it was called the sacred month. In this month Mahommed in his early days used to repair every year to the cave of Mount Hira, and pass the time in prayer; such was the regard paid to it by him that in the second year of his Hegira, he ordered that this sacred month should be observed by his followers as a fast time in imitation of the Christian fast of Lent. To enhance the sanctity of this month, Mahommed declared that the Koran was sent down by God to the lowest heavens in the month of Ramadan on the twenty-seventh night called the night of Power, and moreover that during the month of Ramadan the gates of heaven are kept open, and those of hell are kept closed and the devils are kept chained therein. The Mahommedans to mitigate the rigour of these fasts take a hearty meal just before sunrise, and then soon after sunset have their other meals and give themselves to every kind of luxury after that hour till next daybreak. However it is not infrequently seen in many places, that pious Mahommedans spend a great part of the night also in the exercise of pious practices such as going to Mosques for their prayers, and reading the Koran or sermons. No doubt even this fast as it is practised, is very irksome and severe, especially in hot climates and when the daily occupations are of a severe nature. Ramadan fast is concluded when the new moon again makes its appearance, and that day is kept as a great festival, called the 'breaking of the fast' on which day the Koran commands that alms be given in abundance to the poor. The other day specially observed as a fast day during the year is called Ashura, the tenth day of Moharram, which is the first month of the Moslem year. This whole month is spent in mourning by Shiite Mahommedans in commemoration of the martyrdom of Ali and his sons Hasan and Hussain the Caliphs of Shiites sect. Taboots or Taziahs are constructed of bamboos covered with tinsel and ornamented profusely to represent the tomb of Hussain on the plain of Karbala. Large sums are sometimes spent on these Taboots. At the back of the Taboot are laid generally articles similar to those supposed to have been used by Hussain at Karbala, as a turban of gold, a rich sword, a shield, a bow and arrow. Every morning people assemble round the Taboots, and beating their breasts crying, 'Ali! Ali!' 'Hussain! Hussain!' and go about in procession carrying the usual standard of Moslem, a figure of a hand placed on a pole to represent the five members of the family of the prophet, namely Mahommed, his daughter Fatima, her husband Ali, and their two sons Hasan and Hussain, and also a spear which is called 'Neza,' with a lemon on its top to recall that the head of Hussain was carried on a spear in procession for ten days. On the tenth day the Taboot and the standards are carried in procession amidst crowds of men and boys, who to recall the memory of the confusion and disorder of those days when Hussain was killed, run in various disguises before the procession until they reach an open place near water representing the plain of Karbala. There amidst shouts the spear and lemon are cast into the water. After this a feast is held, known as the Mahorram feast.

The practice of fasts inculcated by Mahommed seems to have been likewise borrowed by him from the Jews who also fasted a whole month from sunrise to sunset, no enjoyments being allowed until after sunset.

The fourth point of religious practice (Din) commanded by the Koran is the *Pilgrimage* to Mecca called Hajj. Before we speak of the time and manner of

performing this pilgrimage, it may be proper to give
a short account of the temple of Mecca, the chief scene
of Mahommedan worship.   We have already seen in
the foregoing chapters that the temple of Mecca
was a place of solemn worship and of singular
veneration among the Arabians for many centuries
before the birth of Mahommed.   Though it was
dedicated at first to an idolatrous purpose, Mahommedans believe that the temple of Mecca is co-eval with
the world and say that when Adam was expelled by
God from paradise, he begged of God that he might
erect a building to worship God, and in answer to his
prayers God let down from Heaven a representation of
the building in curtains of light, and it was set down at
Mecca, and that Adam was ordered by God to turn
towards it while he prayed.   After the death of Adam,
his son Seth built a house of stones and clay in the
same form, which having been destroyed by the
Deluge, was rebuilt by Abraham and his son Ishmael
at God's command in the very place where the former
one stood.   In the course of ages it has undergone
many repairs, rebuildings, and even alterations.   The
most sacred thing in this temple which is called
Kaaba, is the black stone set in silver and fixed in the
south-eastern corner of the Kaaba.   This stone is very
highly venerated by Mahommedans and is called the
right hand of God on earth.   It is considered to be one
of the precious stones of paradise, and it is believed that it
fell down to the earth with Adam when he was expelled
from paradise, and that after the deluge while Abraham
and Ishmael were rebuilding the Kaaba, they, need-
ing a stone to mark the corner of the building Ishmael
went in search of one, when the Angel Gabriel met him
and gave him this famous stone, and revealed its origin to
him.   It is said that at first it was whiter than milk, but
it has become black from the sins of those who touched

it. It is of an irregular oval form about seven inches in diameter. It seems to be of meteoric origin; similar stones may be seen in any great museum. On the northern side of the Kaaba is a little hollow ground lined with marble, where also the pilgrims go to pray. It is said that this is the spot where Abraham and Ishmael prepared mortar for the building of the Kaaba. In another corner there is another stone, also venerated by the pilgrims. This is said to be the stone on which Abraham stood, and which served him as a moveable scaffold while building the Kaaba, and that it rose and fell under his feet as he required and that it still bears the foot-prints of Abraham. It is enclosed in an iron case and the pilgrims are ordered by the Koran to pray before it. The other most important and highly venerated object in Mecca is the Zem Zem well situated on the eastern side of the Kaaba. It is supposed to be the spring that gushed out for the relief of Ishmael when Hagar his mother was wandering with the child Ishmael in the desert. The water of this well is regarded as very holy, and is highly reverenced; it is drunk with great devotion, and is sent in bottles to distant places as a most sacred thing of great rarity. The Moslems make use of it with superstitious belief during illness, apply it to their eyes to brighten their vision and take a few drops of it at the hour of death, and wash the dead bodies with it, and they attribute great efficacy to it.

This sacred Mosque is the one true temple of the Mahommedans, and inasmuch as it contains the Kaaba with its black stone, it has become the central object of Moslem worship, towards which every Moslem has to turn during prayer. Sura II clearly enjoins that *From whatever place thou comest forth, then turn thy face towards the Sacred Mosque, for this is a duty enjoined by the Lord.* It is curious to note that

Mahommed while upholding the unity of God, and His spiritual worship, and whilst so strenuously denouncing all idolatry, should lend himself to the making of this ancient place of Arab idolatry a centre of Moslem worship, and that he should enjoin his followers to regard the anciently venerated objects of Arab idolatry contained within the Kaaba, as objects of the highest veneration and worship for Moslems also.

To this sacred temple every Mahommedan who is sound in health and of full age, and has sufficient means to pay his expenses after duly providing for the support of his house till his return, is obliged to go on pilgrimage at least once in his life, nor are women excused from the performance of this solemn duty. The pilgrimage to Mecca was not introduced by Mahommed. The practice was in vogue among the Arabs before his time and he only made it more binding on his followers slightly amending its practices in the direction of decency.

The pilgrimage must be made in the twelfth month called Dhulhajj *i.e.* ; Lord of the Pilgrimage, a month set apart for the celebration of this solemnity.

As soon as the pilgrims arrive in the outskirts of Mecca, they put off their ordinary clothes, and after performing the ordinary purifications and prayers, put on the Ihram or pilgrim's garb, consisting of two pieces of white cloth, one girding the waist and the other thrown over the shoulders, and with sandals on their feet, and with heads uncovered, recite the prayer, *O God I purpose to make this Hajj, make this service easy to me and accept it from me*, and then reciting aloud the pilgrim's song *Labbeik, Labbeik*, they enter the city of Mecca, and immediately visit the sacred temple and kiss the black stone. They then go seven times round Kaaba, thrice running and four times more slowly, observing each time to kiss the black stone when they pass by it. Then the pilgrim presses his breast and right cheek against the wall of Kaaba, and raising up his arms says, *O Allah, Lord of this ancient house, free my neck from hell fire and preserve me from every evil deed, make me contented with that daily bread which thou hast given me and bless me in all thou hast granted, I beg pardon of Allah and to Him I repent.* Next the pilgrim proceeds to the place of Abraham, and after praying there, has to go to the Zem Zem well and there drink very devoutly some of its water, and then come back and kiss once more the black stone. Next he goes to and fro with his head erect seven times partly at a slow pace and partly running between Mounts Safa and Marwah as one seeking a lost thing in memory of Hagar seeking water for her son. On the eighth day of Dhulhajj the pilgrim has to go to Mina, a place three miles distant from Mecca, and spend the whole night there in devotions. The next morning he repairs to Mount Arafat in a hurried manner. Mahommedans say that in this place Adam found his wife Eve. The legend is that when Adam and Eve were cast out of paradise, Eve fell on Mount Arafat, and Adam in Ceylon. After many years of wandering in search of his wife, Adam found her on this hill, since then called the Mount of Recognition; it is about eleven miles from Mecca. It may not be out of place to make mention here of another legend concerning the gigantic size of our first parents. Mahommedans say that Adam was as tall as a lofty palm tree, and that he has left the mark of his huge foot print on a hill, thence named Adam's Peak in the Island of Ceylon. Eve also was of such enormous size that when she laid her head on the top of a hill near Mecca her legs reached the plain below. Here on Mount Arafat the pilgrims spend a day and a night in prayer, reading the Koran and listening to sermons.

On the tenth morning they all go to the valley of Mina, where there are three pillars representing devils, and each pilgrim has to take into his hands several small stones, of which he throws seven at each of these pillars saying, *In the name of Allah I do this in hatred of the devil and to his shame.* The legend is that when Abraham was tempted by the devil to disobey God's command to sacrifice his son Isaac, he drove the devil away by throwing stones at him. This over, a victim such as a camel or sheep is then slain, and a part of the flesh given to the poor, the rest being dried as a provision for the return journey. After this the pilgrims shave themselves, pare their nails and lay aside the pilgrim's dress. They then once more go to kiss the black stone and to take leave of the Kaaba when with tears in their eyes they in prayer express their regret that they have to depart from a place so dear as the sacred Kaaba is. Thus the Hajj is concluded.

Almost all the above ceremonies were observed as Mahommed himself admits by pagan Arabs, many ages before the prophet's time. The circuits round the Kaaba, running between Safa and Marwah, throwing stones at Mina, were all practices in vogue among the pagan Arabs, and Mahommed the prophet of Islam, the preacher of one God and denouncer of idolatry enjoins on his followers the strict observance of all these pagan superstitions and idolatrous practices.

Another positive precept that is enjoined on Mahommedans is that of *circumcision*, though it is not mentioned in the Koran. Mahommedans hold that it is an ancient divine institution obligatory upon all men. The Arabs used this rite for many ages before Mahommed, having probably learnt it from Ishmael. Moslem divines say that this practice began with Adam himself, who had been taught by the Angel Gabriel to cut off that flesh which, after his fall, had rebelled against his spirit, and hence they draw the conclusion that it is obligatory upon all men to undergo circumcision. Ishmaelites used to circumcise their children when they were about twelve years old, and Mahommedans circumcise their children when they are between six and twelve years old, and when they can say the short Kalima, *There is no God but God, and Mahommed is the apostle of God.*

NEGATIVE PRECEPTS OF THE KORAN

HAVING spoken of the fundamental points of Mahommedanism relating to Iman, (Faith) and to Din (Practice) we must add a few words regarding negative precepts or prohibitions that are enjoined on Mahommedans.

(1) Above all other things Moslems are prohibited the use of any kind of strong and intoxicating *liquors.* The use of opium and of 'beng,' that is, hemp leaves made in pills, is also considered equally unlawful, because it intoxicates and disturbs the understanding.

(2) *Gambling* is likewise prohibited in the Koran. The game of casting lots by arrows much practised among the pagan Arabs was a source of great disturbance and the occasion of much quarreling, and therefore it was solemnly prohibited by Mahommed. Mahommedan divines teach that all games of hazard or chance, such as dice, cards, and such like are comprehended in this prohibition and they likewise consider gaming-houses as places of the greatest scandal and gamesters no better than thieves.

(3) The *divination by arrows* to consult one's luck before undertaking anything of importance is equally prohibited to the Moslems. The arrows of divination were simple arrows, generally three in number, on one of which was written 'God hath commanded' on another 'God hath forbidden' and the third was blank: and the

drawing of one of these arrows decided the question. The Arabs had recourse in all undertakings of importance to this form of divination.

(4) The Koran further prohibits the *eating of blood, the flesh of whatever dies of itself, pig's flesh* and the *flesh of the victims offered to idols* except in case of necessity such as starvation, etc. No doubt this law of prohibition arises from natural aversion to eating the flesh of an animal dying of disease or age. The taking the blood, was a custom among Arabs, who used to draw blood from a live camel or sheep into a gut and boil it and eat it as a black pudding. Swine's flesh the old Arabs seem not to have eaten, as they had some aversion to it. It is not improbable that Mahommed borrowed this precept from the Jews who were forbidden by Mosaic law to eat the flesh of the pig. The Koran says : ' *O ye believers, eat of the good things with which we have supplied you and give God thanks if you are His worshippers, only that which dieth of itself and blood and swine's flesh and that over which any other name than that of God hath been invoked, hath God forbidden you.* Mahommedans are not allowed to eat any flesh meat unless the animal has been killed in Mahommedan fashion, by severing the windpipe and gullet; repeating at the same time ' Bismilla hillahil-Akbar.' ' In the name of God, God is great.' They are not however forbidden to eat with Jews or Christians provided the meat and drink used at the table is of a lawful nature for them ; and in fact the Moslems do not object to eat with Jews and Christians in several countries, though the contrary is the prevailing custom in India.

(5) The law of Mahommed has also put a stop to the inhuman practice of infanticide as long practised by the pagan Arabs, by burying their female issue alive, to save them when grown up, from being either reduced to poverty or falling into disgrace. The birth

of a daughter was considered a great misfortune and all the female children whom they did not want to bring up, were buried in a pit alive. This inhuman custom continues even in our own day in several pagan countries, and until recently in several parts of India. The law of Mahommed did a great deal of good by condemning this inhuman practice. The British law also has done its best to put down this inhuman crime, wherever its influence extends and its laws are obeyed.

(6) *The seclusion of women.* The Koran (sura 24) forbids women to appear unveiled before any member of the other sex with the exception of certain near relatives. It says, '*And speak unto the believing women, that they restrain their eyes, and preserve their modesty, . . . and let them throw their veils over their bosoms (taking care to cover their heads, necks, and breasts) and not shew their ornaments unless to their husbands, or their fathers or their husband's fathers, etc. . . . and let them not make a noise with their feet, (that is let them not move about their feet so as to allow those charms to be seen, which ought to be veiled)* ' This law coupled with other similar restrictions, has led to the complete seclusion of the harem and zenana. While this law tends to keep society in a very low state of civilisation, and perpetuates many customs of semi-barbarism, still when one considers the laxity of the marriage tie among Moslems, the prohibition has the appearance of prudence ; because every married woman may become the wife of any other man whom she may captivate if she persuades her husband to pronounce a divorce. Moslems are therefore compelled to keep their wives closely confined ; hence this prohibition is considered of the greatest importance to the protection of society. For the same reason a similar custom of seclusion prevails among a considerable section of the Hindoos of India, where also the marriage tie is very lax.

Whatever reasons may have originally justified the enforcement of such a barbarous practice, zenana life is really bad for man at all stages of his life, for it not unseldom becomes the nursery of vicious habits, and a fountain from which the young of either sex through mixing freely with the slave members of the harem, imbibe the germs of immorality and of other evil habits. On the whole the seclusion of women exercises a very demoralising influence in the home life and becomes an insuperable barrier to the regeneration and progress of a nation besides keeping society in a stagnant condition.

(7) In the thirtieth chapter of the Koran the practice of Usury is strictly forbidden, and this includes even the taking of any interest for money lent.

All these prohibitions especially those of the use of liquour and opium and the practice of usury, seem to be dead letters in the practical life of the generality of the Mahommedans, at least at the present day.

ISLAM'S INFLUENCE ON SOCIETY

THE Mahommedan religion on the whole with all its dogmatic and moral principles, and with all its positive and negative laws has been a curse to human society. Mahommed pretended to confer by his religion a boon, at least on his own countrymen, by giving them in place of gross idolatry a purer faith, and surer moral habits, but in this attempt he has miserably failed and has hopelessly fallen into the very sin he so vehemently assailed. Mahommedanism has penetrated into barbarous countries and has forced its inhabitants to accept it as their saving religion, but in doing so it has not succeeded in elevating man's condition to a higher level—or at least to a level any higher than that of Arabia in Mahommed's time.

The partial and specious reforms which it may have attempted to effect, are vitiated by the fact that they tend to exclude the higher and nobler virtues; and as the inner life of families, the whole tone of society and the intellectual and moral standard of a people depend on the principles of the ruling religion, it is hopeless to expect that Islam will ever cease to be what it has hitherto proved, the most formidable obstacle to the dawn of a progressive and enlightened civilization. How can it be otherwise? no permanent house can be built on a foundation of sand; what permanent civilization and progress then can be expected from a people professing a religion founded on fatalism, polygamy and slavery? Their blind belief in inevitable fate, and their antagonism to liberty of thought and action have rendered reform next to impossible; and the professors of this religion seem never to realise their obligations and duty towards the people under their rule, of spreading true civilization, good government and the cultivation of the peaceful arts. The natural consequence of this ignorance and blindness has been despotism, mal-administration, bigoted persecution and oppression of their co-religionists.

In the countries of the Mahommedan world anarchy, rapine, revenge, strife and murder are the order of the day; thieving, lying, usury and oppression are looked upon more as virtues than vices; unrestrained licentiousness is carried to unimaginable excess. Dirt and filth are things that never come seriously before the attention of Mahommedans, they seem indeed to prefer living in the most dirty and filthy environment. They are generally illiterate and at the same time self-conceited, and their vainglory in their religion and the nothingness of their own acquirements makes them scorn every other religion; the meagre education which they generally receive when young, makes them

believe that there is not much more left for them to learn
in the world. In short, Mahommedan countries are the
chosen homes of ignorance, bigotry, tyranny and brutal
vice, and a rendezous for a filthy, unprincipled people,
as well as for brigands, felons and freebooters. While
all other countries not influenced by Islam have made
rapid progress in every direction and enjoy the blessings
and peace of true civilization, Mahommedan countries
have remained absolutely opposed to change and reform ;
nay, rapacity and extortion have reduced them to a
most deplorable state.

Such is the boon conferred on human society by
the Mahommedan religion, and what a benefactor
Mahommed has been to his country ! who was pleased
to give to his country, nay, to the whole world,
a religion which, claiming a divine origin as the final
and irrevocable standard of morality, has kept its
followers sunk in ignorance and barbarism, and has
become an insuperable barrier to the regeneration,
civilization and progress of the Eastern world.

THE TESTIMONY OF THE KORAN ON THE OLD AND THE NEW TESTAMENTS

WHILE Mahommedans admit the divine origin of both
the Old and the New Testaments, they charge both the
Jews and the Christians with corrupting their Scriptures
and with suppressing in them the prophetic announce-
ments of Mahommed's advent. When these Mahommedans are asked to prove in what age, by whom,
and in what manner the Scriptures of the Old and
New Testaments were in any way corrupted ; and
when they are told that it is not only simply gratuitous
but ridiculous on their part to make such groundless
accusations, and when they are further challenged
to sift the passages which are authentic from the

corrupt remainder or to distinguish the divine and authoritative from the human and erring they can only assert that whatsoever is at variance with the Koran is, without further argument, to be rejected, because it is a corruption and an interpolation fabricated presumably for the purpose of bolstering up Judaism and Christianity against the superior claims of Mahommed. It is quite superfluous to prove here the impossibility of this corruption of the Old and the New Testaments, because the Old Testament, especially the Septuagint edition, was in the hands both of Jews and of Christians, and as these people were rivals in religion, any attempt on any side to vitiate the genuineness of their Scriptures would have been most vigorously attacked. In like manner the corruption of the text of the New Testament as it was handed down from apostolic times, would be impossible because its perfect genuineness was not only most carefully guarded by holy men from early times, but it was most zealously watched by the enemies of Christianity and any attempt to vitiate its genuineness, or to make any kind of change in its text would have produced a wide clamour and protest from all sides. The Mahommedans further forget that the Old and the New Testaments were already existing for several centuries before the Prophet of Islam was born, and long before his advent copies of the Old and the New Testaments were spread far and wide throughout the greater part of the known world, transcribed in various languages. Mahommed himself was well acquainted with the Jewish and Christian Scriptures and had every opportunity of securing some copies at least of the genuine Scriptures and had he cared so to do could have shewn to the Jews and to the Christians which passages were true and genuine and which had been corrupted. On the other hand the Koran everywhere refers to both the Old and New Testaments, as they were then in existence and in common use, and Mahommed exhorts both the Jews and the Christians to follow the precepts of their respective Scriptures; and from first to last both portions of the Bible are spoken of in the Koran in terms of reverence and homage consistent only with a sincere belief in their genuineness and authenticity. Therefore it must be conclusively assumed that the Jewish and the Christian Scriptures, current and extant at the time of Mahommed, were held by him to be genuine and of divine authority.

In the Koran the Jews and the Christians are ordinarily styled as '*The people possessing the Book, Scripture, Gospel; The people possessing the Admonition or Revelation; Those to whom the Book, Scripture, hath been given; Those to whom We (God) have given the Book.*' These expressions are repeatedly found throughout the Koran and all afford a clear evidence of the belief of Mahommed that the scriptures of Jews and Christians were divinely inspired. The passages corroborating this fact are so frequently met with in the Koran, that it would be quite impossible in the limits of our space to quote them all, however for the satisfaction of Mahommedan readers who make bold to accuse Jews and Christians of having corrupted their Scriptures we quote a few testimonies of their own prophet bearing directly on what we have said above.

Sura XXXII 24: '*And verily We delivered the book of the law unto Moses; wherefore be not in doubt as to the revelation thereof; We ordained the same to be a direction unto the children of Israel.*' (The book referred to is the Pentateuch [Tourat], revealed by God as a code for the Israelites, and Mahommed is here commanded by God not to be in doubt as to the reception of this revelation and the acknowledgement of it as divine). Further Sura VI v. 154: *We also gave unto Moses the book of the law, a perfect rule unto him, who should do right; and a determination concerning all the things needful and a direction and mercy.'* (Here one can see that the divine origin of the Pentateuch is not only affirmed but is praised in the highest terms, as a thing perfect and excellent and as a guide to salvation. Why then should Mahommedans call this book corrupt while their own prophet so highly praises it?) Sura XXI v. 49: ' *And verily We gave Moses and Aaron the distinction (Al Forcan) and a light and an admonition to the pious—those who fear their Lord in secret; and who tremble for the hour of Judgment; This blessed admonition also We have sent down; will ye therefore deny it?* (The Books of Moses (Tourat) here are named *Al Forcan* a distinctive epithet which is equally applied to the Koran itself). Again Sura XVII v. 65: ' *And verily We have bestowed favour upon some of the prophets more than upon others and We gave David the Psalms, (Zabur)* ; and in Sura IV: '*And We have given thee the Koran as We gave the Psalms unto David'*; and further in Sura XXI v. 105: ' *And verily We have written in the Psalms after the promulgation of the law, that my servants the righteous shall inherit the earth, and in this Book are contained sufficient means of salvation unto people who serve God.'* (Here again one can see how Mahommed clearly admits the divine origin of the Psalms [Zabur] as extant and in current use among Jews and Christians, and declares that they contain doctrines sufficient for man's salvation. Nay he puts on the same level the inspiration of the Koran, and of the Psalms.) Further Sura LXI v. 6: ' *And when Jesus the son of Mary said, O children of Israel verily I am the apostle of God unto you, attesting that which is before me of the Tourat and giving glad tidings of an apostle that shall come after me whose name is Ahmad.'*

K

After confirming the authenticity of the Tourat and Zabur as extant among the Jews and Christians, Mahommed quotes this verse as an introductory message of Jesus to the people of Israel. He applies to the Jewish scriptures the word ' Taurat' meaning the whole canon of the Old Testament, which was then complete and definite as it now stands. The second verse in the above quotation seems to refer to the promise made by Jesus of the Paraclete or Comforter, '*I will ask the Father and He will give you another Paraclete, that he may abide with you for ever*' (St John XIV. 16) and Mahommed appropriated it as a promise of himself who was to come, reading Paraclete into Periclyte (meaning illustrious, which is the same as to say ' Ahmed '). A simiiar interpolation is also found in the spurious gospel of St Barnabas made so much of by Mahommedan divines. Again Sura IV 1ô9. '*Verily the Messiah (Christ) Jesus the son of Mary is an apostle of God and His word which He conveyed into Mary and a Spirit proceeding from Him ; Believe therefore in God and in His Apostle.*' Again Sura III 2 : '*He had before this sent down the Tourat and the Gospel for the guidance of mankind.*' Again in the same Sura III 48 : '*When the angel said O Mary verily God sendeth thee good tidings, that thou shalt bear the Word proceeding from Himself. His name shall be Christ Jesus the son of Mary, honourable in this world and in the world to come and one of those who opproach near to the presence of God . . . She answered, Lord how shall I have a son, since a man hath not touched me ? the Angel said so God createth that which he pleaseth . . . And God shall teach him (Jesus) the Scripture, and the Wisdom and the Tourat and the Gospel and shall appoint Him His apostle to the children of Israel and He shall say, verily I come unto you with a sign from your Lord, I will heal the born blind and the leper, and I will raise the dead to life and I will prohesy unto you.'* And again Sura V. 50: *'We also caused Jesus the Son of Mary to follow the footsteps of the prophets, confirming the Scripture of the Tourat, which was sent down before Him; and We gave Him the Gospel containing direction and light, confirming also the Tourat which was given before it, and a direction and an admonition unto those who fear God; that the people of the Gospel might judge according to that which God hath revealed therein and whosoever judgeth not according to what God hath revealed, they are transgressors.'* Sura LXVI. 13: *'And Mary daughter of Imram, who preserved her chastity and into whose womb We breathed of our spirit, and who believed in the words of her Lord, and His Scriptures, and was a devout and obedient person.'* The above quoted passages are the clearest evidence, that according to the Koran, the Scriptures of the Tourat and Gospel, that is the Old and New Testaments, in current use amongst the Jews and the Christians in Mahommed's time, had been revealed by God himself, and therefore were authentic and genuine. Further we may remark what high claims the Koran allows to Jesus, when it recounts his wonderful birth in the womb of the Virgin Mary through the operation of God's spirit, the great power of working wonders with which He was endowed, and that He is glorious, honourable, and one who is to stand near to God, and that He is an apostle of God, sent down to confirm the Scriptures of the Tourat that had been revealed before Him, and that He is to teach the Gospel containing directions, admonitions, and that these teachings are to be held as indisputable rule of judgment and further adds that whoever does not judge according to these revelations, shall be unbelievers and transgressors. Here follow the crowning testimonies; Sura V. 77: *'O ye people, who have received the*

See also page 157

*Scriptures; you are not grounded on anything, until
ye observe the Tourat and the Gospel and that which
hath been revealed unto you from your Lord'*; And
again in Sura V. 60. *We have also sent down
unto thee the book of the Koran with truth confirming
those Scriptures, which were revealed before it,
and a custodian thereof to preserve the same from
corruption.'* These are admirable and indisputable
testimonies by which a fair minded man and even
a candid Mahommedan can see that the genuineness
and authenticity of the Old and New Testaments
have been completely attested by the Koran. Further-
more it solemnly adds that his people who have
received the Scriptures (Koran) have no solid grounds
of faith, their foundation is insecure and insufficient
and their religion is futile, unless they observe and
follow the Tourat and the Gospel; their profession of
obedience to the Koran is nothing so long as they
observe not the Tourat and the Gospel because without
these, their faith is insufficient. Then ye candid
Mahommedans who say that the Scriptures of the
Old and New Testaments have been corrupted, and
are therefore unauthoritative and besides have been
superseded by the Koran, how can you sustain these
frivolous accusations, when you have these words
from your own prophet? Do you forget that in
addition to the Koran he enjoins strict observance of
the doctrines contained in the Old and New Testaments,
because they contain instruction, light and admonition to
mankind? The Scriptures of the Old and the New
Testament in the hands of Christians at the present
day are the same as they were at the time of Mahommed.
All that Mahommed opposed were the new and false
doctrines and traditions that were prevalent among
the Jews and Arabian Christians of his time and
their refusal to acknowledge him as an apostle of

God and a prophet. Further Mahommed enjoins on
his followers a firm belief in and due regard and
veneration to Jesus Christ and invokes a curse from
God on those who should refuse their faith in Jesus.
Sura III says : ' *When God said to Jesus, verily I will
cause thee to die and I will take thee up unto me and I
will deliver thee from the unbelievers and I will place
those who follow thee above the unbelievers until the
day of resurrection . . . Moreover as for the infidels,
I will punish them with a grievous punishment in
this world and in that which is to come. But they
who believe in thee and do that which is right, I
shall give them reward. These signs and this prudent
admonition do We (God) rehearse unto thee (Mahommed).
Verily the likeness of Jesus in the sight of God, is as
the likeness of Adam, (in respect of his miraculous pro-
duction by the immediate power of God), as Adam was
produced out of the dust. This is the truth from Thy
Lord ; be not therefore of those who doubt ; whoever shall
dispute with thee concerning him (Jesus) after the knowledge which hath been given unto them . . . let us then
make imprecations and lay the curse of God on
them.*'

Then, you Mahommedans, read carefully the above
quoted genuine texts taken from your own sacred
Koran and consider well ; and according to these words
of your own prophet, beware lest you ground your faith
on anything without first having due regard to the
Scriptures of the Old and New Testaments ; see
that you are not an infidel who refusing to believe in
Jesus Christ as revealed in the Holy Gospels, become
guilty of the sin of infidelity, liable to terrible
punishment both in this world and the world to come.
But be a true believer in Jesus Christ and thus believing in Him and doing that which is right without any
fear, that is following the true religion taught by Him,

be able to participate in the grand reward promised by
the very Koran, to the true believers and followers of
Jesus Christ, who is the true prophet of God, whose
divine mission He has beyond every doubt, fully proved
both by working wonderful miracles and by the great
sanctity of His most pure life. Again ponder very carefully the true sense of the words 'these signs and this
prudent admonition do we rehearse unto thee.' Here
Mahommed is commanded to preach Jesus Christ, as a
prudent admonition, and Mahommed has truly preached
Jesus Christ, His life and doctrines as embodied in the
Gospels, by ordering on every one the strict observance
of all that is contained in the Holy Gospels and solemnly
declaring that without this, their faith in the Koran
would be useless and groundless. Then ye Moslems,
do not be still blind-folded and fanatic, follow the
advice and admonition of your own prophet, and firmly
believe in Jesus Christ true Saviour of mankind. Follow
then courageously the salutary religion He has taught
and which is embodied in the Holy Gospels and
is expounded to us by His divinely instituted Church,
and thus by doing what is just and right, without any
further fear or human respect avert both the curse
invoked and the terrible punishments threatened by the
very Koran on those who shall not believe and follow
Jesus Christ the true Lord and Saviour of
mankind.

SUMMARY

In the foregoing chapters we have attempted to present
a comprehensive account of the life and work of the
prophet of Islam ; and now we must leave to our
reader the task of forming an independent opinion
of the real value of that life and its motives, and thereby
appreciating at its true value the religion Mahommed

has given to the world—a religion blindly followed by many millions, among whom there is a number of really learned men, in all other respects truly great men, worthy of the world's admiration.

If we carefully and impartially compare the notorious life of the prophet and his religious system; the one purely human, encompassed with the errors of humanity and the other claiming to be of divine origin and the pure word of God, we are forced to the conclusion that the prophet of Islam was an intentional deceiver and hypocrite, whose religious enthusiasm degenerated into culpable deception.

Nevertheless we must allow that Mahommed was really a wonderful man. Born in a barbarous country, with no great education, with little aid from others and with meagre means at his disposal, but with an indomitable will and with an admirable skill, he succeeded in abolishing to a certain degree the idolatry practised in his native land, and in compelling his rude countrymen to accept his religion on his authority. He gave to the world a creed which has exercised a tremendous influence on the world's progress. He is the acknowledged founder of many ruling dynasties who have brought under their sway a great part of the known world and for centuries threatened the peace of nations. His very name, hallowed and invoked at thousands of shrines, is the inspiration of terror on the battlefield. His words are the belief of countless generations and form the code of laws for nations both for this life and the life to come. All these and many other achievements, judging by the standard of human renown, must place Mahommed in the forefront of the great men of the world.

But let us enter a little deeper into the true character of his life and thus display Mahommed in his true colours.

Undoubtedly his life at Mecca, at least up to the time he assumed the title of the prophet of Islam, was at any rate blameless; his domestic conduct was that of a faithful and affectionate husband, whilst his reserved, meditative and sober manner in public had secured him the love and esteem of his countrymen and his life as a hermit in the cave of Hira had gained him a reputation for sanctity.

It may be fairly assumed that his early longings after a more spiritual faith and his searchings after the knowledge of the one true God were earnest and real, but as he advanced in his ideas and speculations, worldly ambition blinded his mental vision, and from the time he announced himself as the messenger of God, taking His Holy Name to suit his evil purposes, he became a wilful and intentional deceiver, and for the purpose of raising himself to supreme power, invented this wicked and blasphemous imposture, which he carried by artful skill to a wonderful success. It is really astonishing how he succeeded in instilling deep into the hearts of his few early followers such a strong conviction and firm belief in his divine mission, and thus secured their attachment to him without hope of temporal benefit, and through scorn and persecution, induced them to stand firmly by him and share with him the persecutions of his enemies, and even to go willingly into exile with him. To a certain extent this can be explained by the fact that the reformed Arabs of his time were ardently looking for a religious teacher who would lead them by the right way to the knowledge of one true God, without disturbing too much their old superstitious practices, and such a one they found in Mahommed.

As we have already given in detail in the foregoing chapters the different phases and particulars of

Mahommed's life and conduct, it is unnecessary to recapitulate them here even in brief. It is sufficient to give a resume of some leading features and principal actions in his life, which will enable an unprejudiced mind to form an opinion of the true character of that life and religion, and judge whether Mahommed really deserves our admiration or the reverse, and whether he is a safe guide, and the religion he taught sufficient to save one's soul.

Mahommed posed as an apostle of God, the seal of the prophets; as the destroyer of idolatry; as preacher of one true God, and the reformer of morals : while his life is marked by innumerable marriages; and great licentiousness, deeds of rapine, warfare, conquests, unmerciful butcheries, all the time invoking God's holy name to sanction his evil deeds, ordering prayers and alms deeds and at the same time propagating Islam everywhere by fire and sword.

God the creator of heaven and earth is infinitely good, all holy and perfectly just and He cannot tolerate anything in the least sinful or unjust; and anyone calling himself even the least friend of God, must not have anything in him that could even in the least displease Him. What purity and eminent sanctity and righteousness are required in a man, that he may have the rare happiness of being chosen by God as His apostle and prophet ! Abraham and Moses whom Mahommed calls great prophets of God were perfectly sinless and every way just men, who led a life of eminent sanctity and holiness; but what can we say about the purity of Mahommed's actions, of the sanctity and righteousness of his life ?

Mahommed says in Sura II, and Mahommedans themselves believe that all the prophets of God have been free from great sins and errors of consequence. How then could Mahommed, scandalous sinner as he was and as he called himself, in the same breath call himself the prophet of God? Mahommed further says the prophets that came before him worked miracles, to prove they were really sent by God; and speaking of himself frankly admits that he had not received such a power from God. Sura XXIX says '*Unless a sign be sent unto him from his Lord, we will not believe; and such signs are in the power of God alone.*' From these words of the prophet, one may clearly see how far his mission was warranted. The power of working miracles is one of the chief testimonies and proofs of a prophet's divine mission, to shew that he is really a man of God, and that he has been deputed by God as His apostle to preach in His name, is confirmed in sanctity and holiness; and the person who works such miracles by the power of God, for miracles in their proper sense, can be worked only by God who is infinitely powerful, or by such holy persons as have received such power from God. The prophet of Islam while confessing that the prophets who came before him, worked miracles, and while frankly admitting that he is only a public preacher, in the same breath makes bold to claim for himself a superiority over them and calls himself the seal of the prophets, although he inconsistently acknowledges that this singular privilege of working miracles that had been given by God to other prophets, had not been given to him! In the whole of the Koran there is not an atom of proof that Mahommed was truly a man of God, and that he had been sent by God, except the prophet's own gratuitous and groundless assertion and self testimony. Mahommedan writers, conscious of this defect in their prophet, that he had worked no great miracles, contend that there is mention made in the Koran of some miracles as having been worked by their prophet, such as the splitting of the moon, the night journey to heaven, and the conversion of Jinns, but there is no proof whatever of these alleged miracles, they are simple gratuitous assertions made by the prophet in the Koran and blindly believed by his devoted followers on the sole authority of the prophet's unsupported assertion. The splitting of the moon like the throwing of the sun moon and stars in the sea on the last day, and the story of the shooting stars as the heaven's artillery used to drive away the devils who approach heaven to listen to the heavenly secrets, are not only absurd, but scientifically ridiculous; and we have already told how when the prophet announced to his followers the ridiculous story of his night journey to heaven, they called it an absurd and incredible thing and were about to abandon him, when Abu-Bekr his blind and fanatic follower, vouched for its truth, saying that if Mahommed had declared it to be so, it must be true, because Mahommed would not tell an untruth. There is also the absurd story of the conversion of the Jinns, groundless as the story of their creation and existence. Such are the ' miracles ' alleged to have been worked by the prophet of Islam and such is the testimony in support of these ' miracles.' Mahommed in Sura XV alleges that Almighty God gave as His reasons for not granting him the power to work miracles in testimony of the validity of his mission, that when God had sent His prophets, empowered to work miracles, the people had impiously laughed at them and therefore in chastisement of this impiety, He had withheld this power from Mahommed, commanding him to stand before the people only as a public preacher. ' *And the people hithertofore accused the messengers of God of imposture and We produced our signs unto them but they retired afar off, from the same . . . Behave thyself with meekness towards the true believers, and say I am a public preacher* ' ; further,

in Sura XX God is made to counsel Mahommed to bear
patiently the people's ridicule for this want of power in
him : ' *Wherefore do thou, O Mahommed, patiently bear
that which they say and celebrate the praises of thy
Lord . . . The unbelievers have said unless he come
unto us with a sign from His Lord* ; *we will not believe
him. Have they not heard the history of the nations
which came before them.*

THE DIVINE INSPIRATION OF THE KORAN

To those who taunted him as being a prophet without
signs, and demanded from him some miraculous proof of
the truth of his claims, Mahommed pointed to the Koran,
alleging its excellence and eminent superiority as a
permanent proof in testimony of his mission. A book
of such excellence, he said, could not be the work
of himself, an ignorant and illiterate man, and therefore
it was a revealed book, the greatest of miracles ; and if
they were not convinced of this truth, no sign however
stupendous would ever have the power to compel their
belief. Sura II says : ' *Will they say he has forged the
Koran? answer Bring therefore two suras like unto
it, forged by yourselves* ' ; Again Sura VII has : ' *Believe
therefore in God and His apostle the illiterate prophet.*'
As we have already said, the Koran is incomparable for
the excellence of its language and the poetry of its
rhythm ; but because of this, it does not follow that
it is the best book in the world, much less. that it is an
inspired or revealed book. In almost every country
and language are to be found one or two books of super-
excellence. In India we have the Kalidasa in Sanskrit,
of unchallenged superiority over any other book in that
language. No Greek poet can be compared to Homer
and no Latin one to Virgil ; and among English poets,
Shakespeare is unrivalled, and so on. Yet who has ever

ventured to attribute any supernatural origin to these
books ? Mahommedans who are generally ignorant
of works in other languages and who seldom take
any pains to investigate or to understand such, take
inordinate pride in their Koran, with its jingling sounds
and poetic rhymes. It is an admitted fact that Mahommed was a man gifted with great talents, and especially
with a vein of poetry. We have already said that
he was a religious visionary, and it is no wonder
that his Koran was written with considerable dignity of
rhythm breathing forth great thoughts and excellent
ideas ; and Mahommed being a master of eloquence,
his language was cast in the purest and most persuasive
style of Arabic oratory, his fine practical genius
exhausting the imagery of nature in illustration of
spiritual truths. All these things however do not go
to prove that Mahommed richly blessed though he was
with natural gifts, was a man sent by God as his
apostle, nor that his Koran is a book revealed or
inspired by God. Why should Moslems set such
a high store on the external structure of their Koran,
in which one cannot find any idea or doctrine more
sublime or excellent than is contained in the other
revealed books, as Tourat, Zabur and Ingil ? On the
testimony of Mahommed himself those books of the Old
and New Testaments are all inspired books revealed
by God. The Koran itself, according to Mahommed,
was sent down, to confirm that which had been already
revealed in the Old and New Testaments, to be the
custodian of, and to preserve these books from corruption (vide Sura V 60). It is further stated that faith
will not avail the disciple in the Koran unless they
observe that which is contained in the Tourat and the
Gospel as revealed by God (Sura V 77). Why then
should not Moslems esteem and venerate these books of
the Old and New Testaments as at least equal with

their Koran? Why should they allow themselves
to be captivated and blinded by the Koran's external
beauty, its language and rhythm, while its real
contents are for the greater part, where not puerile
and revolting, far inferior to the contents of the
truly revealed books Tourat and Ingil? We have
already shown how false was the allegation that
the Old and New Testaments, were corrupted in later
days and are consequently unauthentic; and it is
therefore quite unnecessary to repeat our arguments
on the point.

The Koran which the Moslems maintain is a work
entirely revealed by God, is nothing else but a pure
creation and concoction of Mahommed and of his
accomplices, as we shall see hereafter, and contains in
great part stories taken from Jewish and Christian
scriptures, from several heretical and apocryphal books
that were then in circulation such as the Gospel of
St Barnabas, the Journeys of the Apostles, a recital of
the acts of apostles Peter, John, Andrew and Thomas,
(in which among other things was mentioned that
Christ was not crucified but another in his stead); some
doctrines from the Magians of Persia, as well as several
from the idolatrous Arabs; and to give them a
fresh colour and adapt them to his designs and purposes,
he not only distorted and magnified to an incredible
degree the simple narrations of the Bible stories and
other ordinary doctrines from other sources, but by inter-
pollations and by the addition of fictitious events he
both corrupted the historical authority of several facts
and rendered the whole more a romantic reading
than a record of serious truths or events. We
have already stated that the general design of the
Koran and the one grand idea of Mahommed, was
to unite into one religion the idolators, the Jews, and
the Christians who then peopled Arabia, bringing them

all to the obedience of Mahommed, as the prophet of God.

When we examine the structure of the Koran, more closely it is singular, how few really aphoristic sentences, proverbs or gems of moral truth are to be found in it. Apart from its claim to inspiration, it is by no means a great literary composition. It is rather a mixture of longer and shorter chapters, many of them a mere disconnected jumble of events.

To answer all emergencies and to extricate himself with credit from any perplexing difficulty, it was an excellent and politic contrivance of Mahommed to say of the Koran that it was eternal remaining in the very essence of God and written on the preserved table, and that a copy of it had been sent down by the angel Gabriel to the lowest heaven, whence it was revealed to Mahommed piece-meal, as the exigency of affairs required ; for if he had said that it was sent down to the earth, and the whole had been published at once, innumerable objections might have been made, whenever he was under the necessity of acting in contradiction to what had been previously revealed or when he should have been compelled to find a new revelation to sanction some of his own deeds. There are several passages in the Koran which are contradictory, and learned Moslems obviate any objection on the point by saying that God commanded several things, which afterwards for good reasons were revoked and abrogated ; and further Mahommedans believe that several passages of the Koran once revealed by God as truths to be believed were subsequently abrogated by the substitution of other verses in their stead. In Sura II we read : ' Whatever verses We (God) cancel or cause thee to forget , We bring a better or its like.' As we have said, it is claimed that the Koran is eternal, every word of it emanating from the essence of God. How can one reconcile this with the theory that the contradictions found in the Koran were truths once revealed, but afterwards revoked; or that some passages once made known to the prophet were abrogated and in their place new ones revealed afterwards? What is eternal is unchangeable and immutable and what is written in the eternal preserved table, how can it contradict itself? A man may make mistakes, and may make alterations or corrections but such is not the case with God who is infinite wisdom and cannot contradict Himself; His words and decrees are eternal and cannot be changed. He cannot reveal now one truth to be believed and after a time reveal another truth quite contrary to the former.

Mahommed professed to receive revelations through the angel Gabriel as the exigency of affairs required to suit his purposes. Messages from heaven were freely brought forward to justify his political conduct, equally with his religious precepts; marriage after marriage was performed, wives after wives were added to the harem, women after women to the number of his concubines; battles were fought; wholesale executions and butcheries were perpetrated; vast territories were annexed; and highway robberies and plunders were committed; all under the pretext of the Almighty's sanction, made known to Mahommed in the revelations; nay even baser and meaner actions were not only excused, but were encouraged under the pretended divine approval and command. A special license from God was produced permitting His prophet an unlimited number of wives, and the disgraceful affair with Mary the Coptic slave was justified in a separate Sura of the revelation; while his desirs for the wife of his adopted son and bosom friend Zeid, was the subject of an inspired message from God Himself who is said to have reproached his greatest prophet for his scruples. In all these atrociously impious actions one can judge whether Mahommed was subject to God, or whether Mahommed made God subject to His prophet's desires, allowing him to do anything he liked and granting to everything His approbation. We must unhesitatingly give the inevitable verdict that Mahommed was an erring mortal, in no sense an infallible model of conduct, but a lewd and profligate man, a fraudulent imposter, who in his gross impiety attempted to make God the apologist for his infamous deeds ; and that his Koran, so highly venerated by Mahommedans, is a pure concoction of his own, a rehash of Bible and other narrations with such alterations and additions, as best suited his own purpose, told in poetic rhythms and jingling sounds fit to captivate the ears of unlearned Arabs.

It is to the credit of Mahommed without doubt, that among a people given up to gross idolatry, he should have conceived a vivid perception of the unity of God, and that he should have preached this great doctrine with firmness and constancy. It is likewise true that the Koran preaches the greatness and goodness of God, the sinfulness of man, the necessity of prayer, alms deeds, and penance ; likewise the judgment of all men on the last day, and several other excellent truths and salutary precepts. But to be true it is not enough that a religion contain some real truths and some excellent moral maxims and precepts. No Moslem would acknowledge the Hindu religion to be the true religion though from its sacred books one can draw several noble descriptions of God's greatness and goodness, as well as many beautiful moral precepts. We must enquire at the same time whether all the things contained in those scriptures and enjoined as truths for man's belief are really such as would reflect credit or discredit on God's name.

L

THE AUTHOR OF THE KORAN

WE have now attempted to examine briefly but minutely
the real life of the prophet of Islam and have with
unbiased mind considered the actual value of that
life, and of the Koran in which is embodied the religion
he has given to the world, so blindly and fanatically
followed to-day by over 100 millions. We shall now
consider who may have been the real authors who
compiled the Koran. In Sura XVI we read : ' *When
We substitute in the Koran an abrogating verse, in lieu
of a verse abrogated, the infidels say Thou art only a
forger of these verses ; but the greater part of them
know not truth from falsehood. Say ; thy holy spirit
(Angel Gabriel) hath brought the same down from thy
Lord with truth, that he may confirm those who believe,
and for a direction and good tidings unto the Moslems.
We also know that they say, Verily, a certain man
teacheth him to compose the Koran. The tongue of the
person unto whom they incline is a foreign tongue ;
but this wherein the Koran is written, is the perspicuous
Arabic tongue.*' We see in the first part of this text
how the Meccans attacked and condemned the conduct
of Mahommed and called him a forger and fabricator,
when he attempted to substitute new verses for former
ones, on the plea that these had been abrogated by
God. When Mahommed insisted, as a proof of its
divine authority, that it was impossible for a man
so utterly unacquainted with learning as he himself
was, to compose such a sublime book, the Meccans
replied that he had one or more assistants in the
forgery, and of this charge he himself makes mention in
the second part of the text quoted, at the same time
attempting to refute it with a very plausible and super-
ficial argument such as that the man suspected or accused

of being Mahommed's confederate in the forgery was a foreigner, while the Koran was written in the Arabic tongue; As if such a thing is inconsistent! However traditions and opinions greatly differ as to the particular person or persons suspected. Some are of opinion that two men called Jabar and Yesar, who were well versed in the Pentateuch and the Gospels and great friends of Mahommed, acquainted him with the writings of the scriptures of the Old and the New Testaments and rendered him much help in the composition of the Koran. Others allege that Abdullah Ebu Salab, a very learned Jew and an intimate friend of Mahommed, assisted him in the compilation of his pretended revelations. But the general opinion is that one Salam. a Persian, and Sergius Boheria, a Nestorian monk, were the chief factors in the composition of the Koran; the former belonged to a good family of Ispahan and while still young, had abandoned the religion of his country to embrace Christianity, and travelling into Syria, was advised by a monk of Amuria to go into Arabia. At Kobe in Arabia, Salam fell in with Mahommed, who had repaired to this place before his flight to Medina, and taking a great liking to the prophet became his follower, and it is the common belief that this man, who was very learned and had studied the systems of different religions, and was well acquainted with Arabic, composed the greater part of the Koran, assisted by Sergius the Nestorian monk, also a friend of Mahommed from his youth and with whom Mahommed in his earlier years had had several conferences at Bosra, a city of Syria.

From the answer given in the passage of the Koran above quoted to the objections of the Meccans, that the person alluded to as the helper of Mahommed in the composition of the Koran, was a foreigner and spoke a foreign language and therefore could not be supposed to assist in a composition written in the Arabic tongue, we can conclude that either Salman or Sergius, who both were foreigners and spoke a foreign language was the person hinted at therein. It is not improbable that Warakah Ebn Nowfal and Othman Ibn-Huweirith, who both were cousins of Khadija, the prophet's first wife and as Christians were well versed in Jewish and Christian scriptures (and whom we have already named as the first converts of the prophet, and from whom Mahommed derived much of his knowledge of Jewish and Christian scriptures in the early part of his life), must have given considerable help to the prophet in the composition of the Koran, or at least of some of the earliest chapters of the so-called revelations.

CAUSES OF THE EARLY SUCCESS OF ISLAM

MAHOMMEDANS sometimes adduce the rapid spread of Islam, as a proof of its divine origin and in itself a miracle; but this growth can be readily explained, for Mahommedanism was a religion well suited to the vain-glorious, and self-conceited Arabs, and Mahommed possessed qualities which enabled him to win over and to hold fast such a race. The Arab gloried in his language and Mahommed declared that it was a Divine language; and that the decrees of God had been written in that language from all eternity. The Arab boasted of the traditional practices and customs of the desert, such as murder, predatory war, slavery, polygamy and concubinage; and Mahommed impressed upon all these usages the seal of a Divine sanction. The Arab gloried in the holiness of Mecca and of the extreme sanctity of the Kaaba and the prophet of Islam made Mecca as the one place chosen by God for his favours and towards which alone they should turn

while they said their prayers, and the sacred Kaaba
he affirmed to be the only portal whereby men could
enter into Paradise. In a word he took the Arab people
just as he found them ; and declared all that they did
to be very good, and approved by God. The fancied
revelations of the prophet gratified the vanity of the Arabs
but failed to elevate them to a higher level ; for what
the Arab was in Mahommed's time he is to-day.
Mahommedanism admirably adaptated itself to the
natural disposition of man, especially to the manners and
opinions and vices prevalent among the people of the
East. The Islam was extremely simple, proposing few
things to be believed and not enjoining many or
difficult duties to be performed. Another great reason
for the success of Islam was the hope of plunder and
conquest. The Moslem power under the first four
Caliphs was nothing but a religio-political association
of Arab tribes for universal plunder and conquest under
the holy name of Islam. They taught Moslems
that fighting for religion was an act of obedience to
God and that true Moslems must fight till all people
were of the true religion. To engage in the Holy War
was the most blessed of all religious duties,and conferred
on the combatant a special merit and a place of very
great glory in paradise after death ; and side by side
with conquest and glory was the bright prospect of
spoil and female slaves. Thus on pretext of spreading
the only true religion, the Arabs swallowed up
the provinces lying all around, driving a profitable
business, enriching themselves with the spoils of plunder
and conquest. On the other hand those who were
cowards, and would not willingly go to battle, were
threatened with the wrath of God and a terrible
chastisement in hell-fire. With such hopes and fears
it is not surprising that Moslems became a fanatic
people and that Islam was spread far and wide. It is

preposterous and absurd to assert that the rapid spread of Islam is a proof of its divine origin ; on the contrary that the religion of Islam owed its progress and establishment entirely to the sword is a most convincing proof of its purely human origin.

PART IV

SECTS OF ISLAM

BEFORE concluding this compilation we may consider briefly the different sects of Islam. We have seen how Mahommedanism was spread far and wide carrying before it sword or tribute. The Koran was its one sacred standard, venerated as the uncreated word of God, and followed as the only way of salvation. As long as Mahommed lived, the religion of the Koran was the same everywhere, but unhappily it lacked those fundamentals and principles necessary to ensure its continuing so. Mahommed himself seems to have foretold that his followers would be divided into seventy-three different sects, every one of which would go to hell, except the one sect which would profess the religion preached and professed by Mahommed himself and his companions.

The number of sects however since, has far exceeded Mahommed's prediction, for according to a learned writer, there are at present no less than 150 different sects of Islam, every one of which bases its authority on the Koran.

In the days of Mahommed and his companions, there was no dispute of any kind among of the followers of Islam, if we except small dissensions concerning the appointments of Imams, or rightful successors of the prophet, which were fomented by self-interested and ambitious people. The Arabs who were continually engaged in holy wars of conquest and the spread of Islam, had scarcely any leisure to enter into nice enquiries about the tenets of their religion; but no sooner had the ardour of conquest and love of war abated a little, than they began to examine more closely the different doctrines of the Koran and to give varying interpretations to its texts; whereupon differences of opinion became unavoidable and consequently this gave rise to different sects; each claiming to be the orthodox and thereby entitled to salvation.

All these different sects can be reduced into two general divisions, namely, orthodox and heterodox. The former, by a general name, are called Sunnis or Sonnites, who profess to hold tenaciously to the teachings of the Koran and acknowledge the authority of the Sonna or Traditions which are the sayings and actions of their prophet, subsequently compiled in six books called *Sihah Sittah*; they besides acknowledge the first four Caliphs or Imams as the rightful successors of their prophet. The Sunnis form by far the greater part of the Mahommedan population.

The Sunni sect is divided into four sections, which while they are sound in fundamentals and completely agreed in all dogmas of Islam, differ in some points of law and religion and in some other minor trivialities, each following the interpretation of the Koran and Traditions as expounded by the four great doctors of Islam, Abu Hanifa, Malik, Al Shafei, and Ibn Hambal. Each of these sects has its own oratory or place of prayer round the Kaaba and each has also a mufti or expounder of its particular law at Mecca. The followers of Abu Hanifa, called Hanifites, who are chiefly guided by their own drivate judgment in their decisions, are found in

Turkey, Egypt and Northern India; Shafites and the
followers of the other two doctors who adhere more
tenaciously to the Traditions, prevail in Arabia, Persia
and Southern India; Malikites are dominant in
Morocco, and in other parts of Africa; and Hambalites
who are at present not very numerous are met with in
some parts of Arabia.

The heterodox or heretical sects on the other hand
are those holding contrary and heretical opinions in
fundamental points of faith. Various sects have arisen
since the early days of Islam, but the most prominent
have been these four: the Motazalites, the Sefatians,
the Kharejites and the Shiites.

The Shias or the partisans of the house of Ali, are
the successors of those who revolted against the
primacy and authority of the first Caliph Abu Bekr
and of his immediate successors, asserting that the
Sovereign Imamat or primacy both spiritual and
temporal over the faithful was by divine right vested
in Ali the son-in-law of the prophet, husband of his
dearest daughter Fatima, and in their descendants
through their sons Hussan and Hossein. The followers
of this sect rejecting the authority of the Sunnahs as
held by the Sunnis, adhere to their own traditions.
They maintain that Ali was the first true Imam or
successor of the prophet and call the first three Caliphs,
Abu Bekr, Omar and Othman, usurpers of the rights
and claims vested in Ali by divine right. They are
also called *Imamiyahs*, because they believe that the
Muslim religion consists in the true knowledge of the
Imams or rightful leaders of the true believers, and while
the Sunnis stigmatize them as *Rafizis* or the forsakers of
the truth, they themselves strenuously maintain that they
are right and like the Sunnis claim the title of *Al
Muminun* or true believers. The Shiahs observe the
ceremonies of the Mohurram in memory of Hussan and

Hossein for the whole period of ten days, while the Sunnis observe only the tenth day, which, they say, was the day on which God created the first man Adam. They likewise hold in great veneration their first twelve Imams, namely Ali aud his eleven lineal descendants, the last of whom was Abu Kassim Mahommed or as he was called Imam Mahommed Mahdi, and who is supposed by them to be still alive, though concealed from public eye and who is to come again in the last days of the world to extinguish all disputes among the true believers according to the Prophet's prediction. Some of the Shiah sects carry their veneration for Ali and his descendants to such an extent as to transgress all the bounds of reason and decency. They regard Ali as almost a partaker of divine nature, attributing to him divine properties, and add in their creed 'Ali as the Wali' to signify that Ali is the Vicegerent of God; and their Kalima is as follows, 'There is no God but God and Mahommed is the Apostle of God, and Ali is the Vicegerent of God.' Their religion consists chiefly and solely in the knowledge of the true Imam. They cling very tenaciously to the teachings of the Koran and repudiate the canonical authority of the six books of the Sonnas or the Traditions held sacred by the Sunnis, considering them to be apocryphal and unworthy of any credit. They have however their own collections of the traditions, which they have reduced into five books. They further accuse the Sunnis of corrupting the Koran and of neglecting to observe its precepts. The sect of the Shiites in short has caused the greatest schism and division in the religion of Mahommed and which to a great extent may be compared to the destruction and havoc caused to the religion of Christ and to His Church by the so-called 'reformation' in the sixteenth century.

The Shiah sect is sub-divided into five principal sects, without counting the innumerable other sects that have sprung from these, so that some consider that Mahommed's prophecy of the seventy-three sects is fulfilled in the Shiites only. Among these five chief sects, the most important one is that derived from Zeid the great-grandson of Ali, known in Moslem history as the Zeidians.

Side by side with this sect of Shiites there sprang up soon after the death of the prophet innumerable other heretical sects mutually branding one another with infidelity. The most important among these are Motazalites, Sefatians and Kharejetes. We shall say a few words about each of these sects.

The Motazalites are the followers of Wasal Ebu Ata who about the 37th year of Hejra broached another heterodox opinion, which rejected all eternal attributes of God, and avoided the distinction of persons made by the Christians ; saying that eternity is the proper and formal attribute of God's essence. They denied absolute predestination, holding that God was not the author of evil, but of good only ; and that man was a free agent. They likewise denied all vision of God in paradise by the corporeal eyes and rejected all similitudes applied to God ; and also rejected the doctrine that the Koran was the eternal and uncreated word of God. This sect has subdivided itself into over twenty different minor sects. The most remarkable of these are (1) the Hodeilians, or the followers of Hamdan Abu Hodeil a Motazalite doctor. (2) The Jobbajans or followers of Wahhab Jobbai, this sect denies that God could be seen in paradise without the assistance of the corporeal eyes. (3) The Hashemians the followers of Abu Hashem, who among other things, were so afraid of making God the author of evil, that they would not allow him to be said to create an infidel, because they said an infidel is a compound of infidelity and man ; and God is not the creator of infidelity. (4) The Nodhamians or the followers of Ibrahim al Nodham who said that the Koran was not an uncreated thing, but a created thing and who in order to disprove the doctrine that God was the author of evil, said that God had no power to do evil : (5) The Hayetians, so named from Ahmed Ebn Hayet ; this sect said that Christ was the eternal Word incarnate and took a true and real body and will judge all creatures in the life to come ; that there is a successive transmigration of a soul from one body into another, and that the last body will enjoy the reward or suffer the punishment ; and that at the resurrection God will not be seen with the bodily eyes, but with those of the understanding. (6) The Jahedhians from Amru Ebn Jahedi, a great doctor of the Motazalites, who said that the damned will not be tormented eternally in hell, and that the summary of man's belief was that God was his Lord and Mahommed the apostle of God. (7) The Mozdarians so named from Isa Ebn Mozdar who affirmed that not only was God the author of evil, but that evil was also to be found in God. (8) The Basharians who carried man's free agency to an excess and taught that God was not obliged to do what is best. (9) The Thamamians followers of Thamama Ebn Bashar who taught that at the resurrection all those who are not followers of Mahommed, will be reduced to dust. (10) The Kadarians who deny absolute pre-destination, saying that evil and injustice ought not to be attributed to God, and that man is free to do as he wills. They are called Kadarians because they deny ' al Kadr ' or God's absolute decree.

The Sefatians hold the opposite opinion to the Motazelites in respect to the eternal attributes of God, which they affirm, making no distinction between the essential attributes and those of operation, and hence they were named Sefatians or Attributists. This sect has branched out into other different sects, the most important of whom are (1) The Asharians who professed the attributes of God to be distinct from His essence, and that no comparison can be allowed between God and His creatures; (2) The Moshabbehites who allowed a resemblance between God and His creatures, supposing God to be a figure composed of parts either spiritual or corporeal, capable of local motion : (3) The Keramians or Corporealists, who not only admitted a resemblance between God and created beings, but declared God to be corporeal; (4) The Jabarians who are the direct opponents of the Kadrians, denying free agency in man and ascribing his actions wholly unto God ; (5) The Morgians who teach that the judgment of every true believer, who has been guilty of a grievious sin, will be deferred till the day of resurrection.

The Kharejites or revolters, revolted from Ali after they had fought under him, because Ali referred a matter concerning the religion of God to the judgment of men, whereas they said the judgment in such case belonged only unto God ; and went so far as to declare Ali guilty of infidelity and to curse him on that account. They further affirmed that any man provided he was pious and just, might be promoted to the dignity of Imam. This heresy and revolt which was instigated by one Khawarej at the head of about four thousand followers was almost entirely destroyed by Ali ; but a few escaped the general destruction fled to different places and there propagated their heresy. Several sects have sprung from them, the chief among them being that started by one Al Waid, known as Waidians, who taught that it was lawful to resist the Imam, when he transgresses the law and that who ever is guilty of a grievous sin ought to be declared an infidel or

apostate. Some of the followers of this sect considered
even the stealing of a grain of corn to be a grievious sin
and that whoever did so, should be pronounced as
an apostate and a reprobate.

Thus far we have treated of the chief sects among the
early Mahommedans. We may now enter more fully
into the history of the great schism, which has separated
Mahommedans into two great factions to this day, the
Sunnis and Shiites, which continue to entertain towards
each other an implacable hatred, while other great
heresies have more or less disappeared or become
merged into some other sect. Though the difference
arose at first for political reasons, it has notwithstanding been so aggravated by additional circumstances and by the spirit of contradiction, that each
party detests and anathematizes the other as abominable
heretics and they regard each other as their worst enemies.
As an illustration of the bitter ill-feelings existing
even to this day wherever the followers of these
two sects happen to live in proximity, we may
quote a small incident that occurred lately among
the hill tribes inhabiting the north western frontiers
of India, and mentioned in the Bombay *Advocate*
of 15th August 1900. Incessant quarrels and
feuds between the two Rahzai clans, led to a conference
in which a thousand tribesmen met in jirga. Many
important disputes were settled. During the meeting
the elders of the jirga pointed out the futility of the
quarrels between these two Shiah tribes, which was
robbing them of the pick of their manhood and
suggested that it would be better to turn their energies
against their Sunni neighbours. Whereupon a member
of the conference left the jirga and shot a Sunni of
another tribe within a few hundred yards of where the
jirga was sitting; but was in turn shot dead himself.
Such is the order of the day, where members of these

two sects live together under a government not strong
enough to maintain order. As we have said the Shiites
reject the Imamship of Abu Bekr, Omar and Othman,
calling them usurpers and intruders; and place Ali on
the same level with Mahommed; they reject the six books
of Sonnas as apocryphal and charge the Sunnis with
corrupting the Koran and neglecting its precepts,
while Sunnis accuse the Shiites of doing the same.
These disputes are the cause of the antipathy which has
long reigned between the Turks who are Sunnis and
the Persians who are Shiites.

In succeeding centuries various impostors from time
to time started up, claiming to be apostles of God and
messengers sent by God to preach the unity of God, and
to publish new laws to mankind, hoping to succeed in
their impostures as Mahommed had done, but most of
them came to nothing. A few, however, made a considerable figure and propagated new sects which
continued sometimes long after their decease. In like
manner in later times several Mahommedan doctors
originated conflicting and mostly heretical movements,
among which the Wahhabi movement was the most
powerful and is yet by no means extinct, though shorn
of much of its former influence. It was founded by
Abdul-Wahhab, who was born in Nejd in Arabia
in 1691 and in his early days was brought up as a
Hahabalite Sunnis. When he grew up, he went on
a religious tour, visiting several places including Mecca,
Bussorah, Bagdad, and Medina, making a study of the
various religious systems that prevailed in these places
and carefully observing the religious practices of the
different sects of Mahommedans.

On his return home, he started a reformation, calling
himself a religious teacher, and animated with zeal for
primitive Islam and with hatred for the extravagances,
excrescences and evils he had remarked in various

Moslem sects, he began to affirm that the Moslem
religion as in vogue at that time had departed
from the primitive doctrine and precepts inculcated
by the Koran. He preached that what is taught by the
Koran was to be strictly believed and that the Koran
should be the sole guide for each man's salvation ;
he rejected the teachings of the Traditions as unfounded
except those which had been derived from the companions of the prophet and claimed the right to private
judgment in the interpretation of the Koran and the
genuine Traditions. He abolished the invocation and
worship of saints and of the dead, and forbade strictly
the use of intoxicants and even of tobacco and likewise
condemned the wearing of gold and silver ornaments.
He condemned the excessive reverence paid to Mahommed and denied his mediation even on the last
day. The use of the Moslem rosary to count the names
of God was forbidden by him, though he attached great
merit to the counting of the ninety-nine names of God
on the fingers. The Mosques were stripped of their
silk and valuables ; and the tombs were desecrated.
He forbade the use of prayers at the tombs even at
those of *pirs* or Moslem saints. He used to say,
' They run there to the tombs to pay the tribute of their
prayers. By this means they think that they can satisfy
their spiritual and temporal needs. From what do they
seek this benefit ? From walls made of mud and
stone, from corpses deposited in tombs. The true way
of salvation is to prostrate oneself before Him who is
ever present and to venerate Him.' He with a companion by name Ibn Saood began a career of conquest
and extended his kingdom all over Arabia. To encourage
his followers to fight boldly and courageously, he used
to give on the day of battle to each soldier a letter
addressed to the Treasurer of Paradise. It was enclosed in a bag which the warrior hung round

his neck. The soldiers were persuaded that the souls of those who died in battle would go straight to heaven, without being examined by the angels Munkir and Nakir in the grave. The Wahhabis soon made themselves masters at Mecca and Medina, where they desecrated many of the sacred places as well as the Kerbela; and the sacred tombs of the Shiite Caliphs; destroyed the golden dome on the tomb of Hosein and committed much other destruction. All the usual pilgrimages were suspended in consequence except for those who were the followers of Wahhabi, and this state of things continued till the Wahhabi dominion was practically crushed and their capital Deraich was destroyed by the Turks towards the beginning of the nineteenth century. Kerbela is the most holy place of the Shiites, having the tomb of Hosein the son of Ali. They believe that whoever lives or dies there, will have nothing to fear in the world to come; and many Shiites leave instructions in their wills that they shall be buried there. Besides the numerous caravans bringing dead bodies for burial, Kerebela is visited every year by numerous pilgrims. Though it seemed crushed the Wahhabi sect soon revived and making Riad in Nejd its stronghold tried gradually to extend its kingdom, though it could never regain its former supremacy. One of its teachers by name Seyyid Ahmed, a freebooter of Bareily in India and said to be a descendant of the prophet, propagated Wahhabi doctrines in India and proclaiming himself the true Caliph or Mahdi commenced a religious war in the beginning of the nineteenth century. To this day the Wahhabis exercise a powerful influence in Northern India.

The other important religious movement that took place among the followers of Islam, is that of Sufiism, which started about the twelfth century of the

M

Christian era. Sufiism is a Moslem adaptation of the
Vedanta Hindu philosophy, allied with the philosophy
of Buddhism together with some doctrines and practices
borrowed from the early Christian anchorites. Their
leading doctrines are : 'God alone exists and is in all
things and all things are in Him. All beings are an
emanation from Him and are not really distinct from
Him. There is no real difference between good and
evil, all being from and in God, who fixes man's
actions. The soul existed before the body, in which it
is constrained, and longs to be set free by death to
return to the Divinity.' Thus we see that Sufiism is
really a form of pantheism. It is not true Mahommedanism, but a structure built on it. The principal
occupation of the Sufis is meditation on the Unity of
God, the remembrance of his names, etc., so as to
obtain absorption. Some Sufis practise the most
severe austerities and mortifications ; they are most
numerous in Persia, and a few are also found in India.

The Sufis are divided into innumerable sects, which
find expression in the many orders of *Fakirs* or
Darwashes. The Arabic word Fakir means 'poor,'
that is poor before God, not necessarily meaning poor
in a worldly sense, and the Persian word Darwesh
means 'door' to signify those who beg from door to door.
Both terms are in general use for those who lead a
religious life. They are divided into two great classes,
those who follow the Mahommedan law to some extent
and are known as *Ba-Shara* (with the law) and those
who while calling themseves Musulmans, care very
little to observe the law of Mahommed, and are called
Be-Shara (without the law). They call themselves
Sufis, because they devote their lives to contemplation
and to religious practices. Maulvis or dancing
darveshes deserve passing remark, their ceremonies
forming a very picturesque sight ; the particular

ceremony or act of devotion common to all classes of darveshes is the *Zikr* or the repetition of the names of God in many different ways. It is a sort of physical exercise, depending upon the lungs and muscles. There are two classes of this Zikr, one recited loud, and the other performed with a low voice, and each is divided into several Zarbs or stages ; for instance, the third Zarb or stage of the low prayer consists in repeating the words ' La-il-la-ha ' with each exhalation of the breath and ' Il-lal-la-ho ' with each inhalation of the breath and as it is performed hundreds of times, it is most exhausting, but proportionately meritorious.   The meaning of these two words is ' there is no deity but God.' Some of the Fakirs are sincere, but others are like many of the Hindu Sannyasis, lazy men who dislike to work and many of whom are grossly immoral.

Before concluding we must not omit to mention the latest movement started by some cultured Muslims of English education, who have formed a new and modern school of Mahommedan thought, resembling to some extent the opinions of Motazalites of old days ; they are called *Freethinkers of Islam*.   These men entirely deny the doctrine of the eternal nature of the Koran, and therefore deny fhe standing miracle of Islam. They hold much more reasonable views on the doctrines of inspiration, disarding the orthodox view of verbal inspiration, and maintain that polygamy and slavery were allowed under the Koran only as temporary measures.   There is a growing body of these educated and cultured Musulmans both in India and elsewhere, who have practically given up the whole code of Mahommedan canon law based on traditions and the too literal interpretations of the Koran given by the greater doctors and writers of Islam, and ignoring everything not found in the Koran, they say they have no other teacher nor code of laws except their prophet Mahommed and his Koran.

Though the Mahommedan religion is fast decaying from its original simplicity, it is still the established and state religion of the whole Turkish empire; including Arabia, Syria, Asia Minor, Kurdistan, Turkistan, Tartary, and the Egyptian provinces, as well as Morocco, Afghanistan, Beluchustan, and some central and western states, where it is very powerful under despotic and almost fanatic rulers. It is likewise strongly represented in India, in Bengal, the North-West Provinces, and the Punjab, numbering about sixty millions and possessing many magnificent mosques and mausoleums, such as the Jumma Musjia at Delhi, and the Taj Mehal at Agra. Even in Benares the great centre of Hinduism, there are over three hundred Mahommedan mosques. Mahommedanism is also strongly represented along the north-east coast of Africa; in the Malaya peninsula, in the Moluccas and the Philippines, and even in China.

The Sultan of Turkey is reputed to be the only true successor to the Caliphs and bears the title of 'Successor of the Prophet.' But he is very much under the control of the '*Ulemas*,' the Mahommedan clergy, who constitute a spiritual hierarchy of despotic power and exercise an enormous influence. They are headed by *Sheik-ul-Islam* or the grand *mufti*, who is nominated by the Sultan as his deputy in the *Imamate*, chosen from among the Mollahs or Superior Ulemas; once nominated he assumes supreme power and from his judgment on matters of law and religion there is no appeal. The conservative and dilatory spirit of the Ulemas of Constantinople is one of the greatest obstacles to any real reformation among the Turkish people.

A few further words about the death and burial of Moslems. The Koran teaches that the hour of death is fixed for every one : and in the Traditions Mahommed teaches that it is sinful to wish for death. When a Moslem is about to die, some skilled reader of the Koran is sent for, that he may read the 36th chapter to tranquilise the soul. The Mahommedan Creed is also said aloud by all present. Early burial is the rule in Islam ; the sooner the dead are buried the sooner they are believed to reach heaven ; while the bad man must be buried quickly that his lot may not fall upon his family. The burial service is believed to be based on the practice of Mahommed. It may properly be recited by the nearest relative, but is usually led by the family Imam or the Cadi. It is said in a mosque or in some open space, and includes many of the ordinary prayers, with a special prayer for the soul of the deceased : after which the people say 'It is the decree of God,' to which the chief mourner replies, 'I am pleased with the will of God.' After this the body is placed on its back in the grave, with the head to the north, and the face turned towards Mecca ; the words of burial being, 'We commit thee to earth in the name of God and in the religion of the prophet.' On the third day after burial it is usual for the relations to visit the grave and recite selections from the Koran, the whole of it being sometimes recited by the Mullahs paid for that purpose. Funeral processions are as a rule made on foot and it is a meritorious act to carry the bier. This is done at a quick pace, that the righteous may arrive soon at happiness. There can be no doubt that the Moslem believes seriously in a future life and state of rewards and punishments but his idea of paradise is usually very material, it being easy to gain by a strict observance of ceremonial, and of outward acts of religion.

We shall end by summarizing the characteristic features of Mahommedanism in the words of a distinguished German scholar who thus writes : 'A Prophet without

miracles; a faith without mysteries; and a morality
without love; which has encouraged a thirst for blood,
and which began and ended in the most unbounded
sensuality.'

We most confidently place this book before the sixty
millions of Mussulmans who are in India * following
blindly one who while he proclaimed himself prophet
of God, gave not the slightes proof of his divine mission
either by the working of miracles or by the sanctity and
purity of his life, which was rather a life of the greatest
wickedness, of heart-rending cruelty and of unbounded
sensuality; The religion of Mahommed was founded
on human passions; it encourages fatalism, despotism
and sensualism; it reduces humanity into unutterable
degradation and it gives no guarantee for the
after happiness of one's immortal soul.   It is on behalf
of these sixty millions of Mussulmans in India that this
little book has been compiled, and it is our earnest
prayer that at least the well-educated and enlightened
Mussulmans may read this book with unbiased and
unprejudiced minds.

* About fifty millions of these are Sunnis, though even among
these as we have said are innumerable minor sects differing from
one another; about four millions Shiites; about two millions
belonging to the reformed sect of Wahhabis and the rest
belonging to various other sects.

CONCLUSION

(A FAMILIAR AND FRIENDLY TALK)

My dear friends and countrymen, the Mahommedans of India,—I repeat again here in these concluding pages, what I have stated in my Preface, that it is not with any intention of insulting the great prophet of Islam, or of offending you his ardent followers, or of vilifying his religion, that the foregoing pages have been written ; but with the sole object of convincing you that the leader you have chosen to follow and the religion you have embraced to obtain your souls' salvation, are unsafe.

Again I entreat you, as your sincere well-wisher, to read carefully these pages, not through your own glasses tainted with illusory doctrines of the Koran, nor through my glasses, which you may perhaps think are selfish ; but with your own clear eyes, with a mind unprejudiced and unbiased, and do not be afraid of any consequences, that may necessarily follow from the careful reading and serious consideration of the matter contained therein.

The sole object for which we embrace a religion and follow its doctrines and its precepts, however hard and unpalatable they may seem to our perverse human nature, is to procure our eternal happiness; and if a religion, however dear it may be to us, cannot serve this end, it must be thrown away, as we would do with any instrument that is found not fit for the purpose for which it was intended.

Mahommed says that there is only one God, and we Christians profess the same thing. If God is one, the true religion cannot be more than one ; for religion is the form by which we worship God, who being eternal truth, cannot be indifferent to the contradictory religions or forms by which He is worshipped ; and further, if He has condescended to reveal from on high a definite religion, surely He cannot be indifferent whether this definite religion which He has revealed, is believed, or some other religion which is in open opposition to it, is professed.

Mahommed in the Koran clearly professes that Taurat *i.e.* Book of Moses or Pentateuch, (Sura XXXII 24 ; and XLV 16) Zabur *i.e.* Psalms of David (Sura XVII 55) and Ingil *i.e.* Gospels (Sura V 50) were revealed by God and that they contain the word of God and an admonition and direction to mankind. Taurat and Zabur besides containing admonitions and doctrines, also foretold the birth, life and death of Messiah (Jesus) ; and the Ingil for the most part contain the narration of the birth, the life and the death of Jesus. Mahommed himself professes the virginal birth of Jesus, shews a very great regard to Him ; calls Him prophet and apostle of God. (See Sura V 119.) Unhappily the death of Jesus Christ on a cross was a stumbling block to the mind of Mahommed, and so in the Koran by rejecting the death of Jesus Christ on the cross, and by saying that only one in his likeness was crucified, he clearly contradicts the Ingil, which clearly say that Jesus Christ was crucified and which Ingil, Mahommed himself professes to be the revealed word of God. It is through the death of Christ, that we Christians hope for pardon and eternal salvation. Jesus Christ is the way, the truth and the life ; there is no other way to heaven but through Jesus Christ.

Mahommed clearly says (Sura XLII 11) that he himself is not an innovator nor a preacher of any doctrine other than that revealed by God to Moses and Jesus, which alone should be observed as a guide to heaven, and that until men observe the doctrines contained in Taurat and Ingil, their faith is founded on nothing (Sura V 77) and that the Koran has been given by God as a record to guard the revealed truths from any corruption (Sura V 56). Here your prophet clearly says that the religion revealed to Moses and Jesus and taught by them is the true religion and the way of salvation and without observance of this revealed religion, all other faiths are of no avail. What further do you need to save your soul in the face of this testimony of your own prophet ? The simple allegation made by Mahommed and his followers that the Ingil, the revealed word of God, had been subsequently corrupted by the Christians, was a thing that neither the prophet nor his followers could ever prove ; and this gratuitous allegation has been completely answered and refuted in the foregoing pages (see page 142.) Neither Mahommed nor his followers, nor any enemy whatever of the true sacred scriptures has ever substantiated such imputations. On the other hand Mahommedan divines themselves confess that the Koran has undergone changes and in several parts has been corrupted. How can it be otherwise, when we remember the history of its compilation ? The Ingil which is truly the word of God has been preserved from such corruptions and it really contains the revealed doctrines taught by Jesus Christ.

My dear friends : earnestly study then the Ingil with a short prayer to God for His grace of light and guidance ; with a calm mind compare the sinless life of Jesus, His spotless purity, His meekness and charity,

His sublime doctrines and His holy precepts, with the sensual life of Mahommed, carried to every excess by his encouragement of concubinage and immorality both by example and law ; his thirst for plunder and blood; his innumerable cruel revengeful butcheries, and many other abominable deeds.   More execrable still was it, to assert that the infinitely good God concurred with him in these iniquitous deeds ; to pretend that God sanctioned such horrors and to adduce God's pretended revelations in support of his wickedness, however revolting and subversive such may have been. The God of infinite goodness and truth to be thus ridiculed, reviled and blasphemed ! ! !

The life of an apostle of God, of one who poses as a prophet, should not bring disgrace to the sanctity of God, as God is all Holy and all Just, so His apostle must be a good and righteous man.   Suppose our King Emperor sends a viceroy to India, and this viceroy leads an abominable and scandalous life, commits acts of tyranny and injustice, indulges in plunder and murder, and makes iniquitous laws ; should he further make bold to say that the King Emperor approves of all his deeds ; how would such a life and such wicked deeds reflect on our own good and just King Emperor ! How then can anyone think otherwise with God who is infinitely good and just.   Accordingly my dear friends, you yourselves can pass your opinion about Mahommed, the so-called prophet and apostle of God.   Further Mahommed says that Moses, David, and Jesus were great prophets of God.   How holy and pious each of these were ! and still Mahommed makes bold not only to place himself on a par with them but he calls himself greater than and superior to them, the Seal of prophets : what greater pride and folly can be imagined ! !

Further, an apostle of God must prove his mission by working miracles. Now compare the proofs which

Jesus Christ gives of His Divine mission, with the proofs which Mahommed can adduce in support of his apostolate. The life of Jesus on earth abounded with astounding miracles. The Koran itself testifies to this (Sura V 120.) Almost every page of the Ingil record more of His wonders; He made the deaf to hear, the lame to walk, the blind to see, and the dumb to speak; He healed diverse persons of long standing diseases and cured lepers with a word only. Before Him the sea became calm, devils trembled; he multiplied five loaves of bread and fed 5000; and He raised the dead to life, one of whom had been four days buried in the grave, and all this by one holy word of His sacred mouth; and in fine the greatest miracle is He Himself risen from the dead after he was in the grave for three days. Now let Mahommed bring forward some of his miracles; if we were to exclude the manufactured miracle of his pretended journey to heaven of which there was no single witness to bear testimony and which his own followers refused to believe until Abu Bekr to save the honour of the prophet, asked them to believe and thus forced them to swallow this bitter pill; there would be nothing worthy of the name of miracle recorded in his life. Mahommed himself candidly confesses that the power of working miracles had not been conferred upon him, while he admits that Jesus Christ was given this power and that Jesus did work great wonders; and still Mahommed has the audacity to say that he himself is a greater prophet than Jesus. It is indeed very wonderful that Mahommed could force God to sanction his ignoble deeds and force God's revelations to authorise the perpetration of his innumerable horrible actions and still he could not obtain from God the power to work miracles. The reason is clear : what an impostor ! ! !

My dear friends,—Please do not be offended; I fully

understand that my talking thus about your revered prophet may displease you. But facts are facts. Is it because you chance to have been born and bred up in the religion of Mahommed? That is not your fault. A person guilty of a crime would not like his crime to be talked about, but if the crime is not any way imputable to him, he would not care, suppose a man to be unwittingly in possession of a wrongful thing or of a deadly poison, or if without knowing it he takes service under someone who happens to be his own deadly enemy; when he discovers his mistake, if he is a man of sense and respects himself and has his own good at heart, he will at once retreat from his false position, however much it may cost him to do so.

Now, do you understand that Mahommed is not the proper leader to follow in preference to Jesus Christ? You have now a true idea of his life and you understand what kind of a person he was and how immoral and wicked some of his religious teachings are. Unless you wish to close your eyes to reason and to harden your heart, you have no excuse for continuing in his deceptive service; if you are really earnest about securing the eternal happiness of your immortal soul, you cannot obtain it by following the lead of Mahommed and adhering to his religion.

I understand that numberless difficulties will stare you in the face, difficulties which would appal and unnerve a man of less force and of weak mind. I understand that a man less courageous might succumb before undertaking the really heavy task of changing the religion in which he has been born and brought up, in which he finds every freedom to lead a life according to his own inclinations, in which he finds full scope for every kind of enjoyment, a religion which offers so many advantages in worldly position. To change such a religion to follow Jesus Crucified; to follow a religion that demands self-denial and requires its followers to lead an honest and virtuous life and to be humble children of the Church founded by Jesus Christ to teach all mankind; what a change is this! This is heroism. You will encounter still more and perhaps very formidable obstacles; you may have to abandon the nearest and dearest members of your family, who perhaps will do their utmost to hinder you with many arguments and inducements. You must further give up those enjoyments and excesses, which are inconsistent with the doctrines of Jesus Christ, and still further, you may have to sacrifice some of your wealth. Now what will be your attitude when you are placed in such a position? Suppose your doctor advises you, to save the life of your body, that it is necessary your leg or hand be amputated which of you will refuse to undergo such an operation? To save the life of the body, which after all will have to die sooner or later, you are ready to undergo such an operation and make no serious difficulty, and none of your friends dissuades you. Then what difficulty can a sane man make when it is a question of saving the eternal life of his soul? What can be more important and more momentous to you, than to save your soul? what loss of advantages and riches can be compared to the loss of everlasting happiness? Is it not worth sacrificing everything to save your soul? Can you lack courage, can you shrink before any obstacles, when the question of saving your soul is concerned? What will it profit you, if you were to gain the whole world, with all its riches and powers and then die miserably and be condemned to the never-dying flames of hell? This world and its pleasures are all illusive and transitory; though for a time they may seem to make you happy they vanish away like the sweet smell of a perfume.

You may perhaps say to me, who has ever seen the happiness of heaven or the flames of hell? who knows in truth what really happens after one's death? Well, do you believe that you have an immortal soul? If you are not entirely a materialist, you will at least say 'I doubt.' Now in doubtful things, it is possible that either both the things doubted turn out to be false, or that one of them turns out to be true. Now we possess a life-giving agency or principle which gives life to our body and which we call the *Soul*, which inasmuch as it is intellectual is absolutely distinct from the life-giving agency which we find in the lower animals. Now this soul which vivifies your body either will cease to exist after death or it will continue to exist. Suppose after your death you should find that your soul really continues to exist and seeks its happiness; what will then be its fate? where is your chance of un-doing the evil done? You cannot come back to your body and undo the evil you have done to your soul in not securing its eternal happiness. Further, suppose it is found true that there is a place after death of eternal bliss or of eternal misery awaiting your soul; what will then be your misery if you have not tried to secure the happiness of your soul in accordance with the laws laid down by its Creator? What will it profit a man if he gains the whole world and suffers the loss of his own soul? Would it not be better in all these doubts and probabilities, to stand on the safest side and on the most secure ground especially when it is a question of such importance and magnitude as the salvation of our soul and the safeguarding of its eternal happiness.

Do not be deluded by another equally dangerous fallacy and say to yourself: Since there is such a conflict among so many religions each claiming divine revela-tion and all truth, I had better hold fast to the one in which I was born and which besides contains several sublime doctrines, and provided I live an honest and righteous life and adore my Creator from my heart, I shall be saved.

I have already shown to you that if God, who is all truth, has condescended to reveal a definite religion, by which He desires to be worshipped, and by which one's soul is to be saved, He cannot be indifferent to what religion He is worshipped by ; and though the worshipper leads an honest and righteous life, still this would not make him fit for the reward of God whom he has not served with due and proper worship. An upright and just man may be an ornament to the society in which he lives, but he cannot on that account alone, be called a loyal subject of his king, or merit that king's good pleasure, unless he also keeps all the laws of the king, and observes faithfully all the formalities and the particular rules of the etiquette by which the king desires himself to be honoured and respected by his subjects.

We have shown (and added to our proofs the testimony of your prophet Mahommed), that Jesus Christ is the true Apostle of God and that His religion is the only way of salvation. Jesus Christ alone has proved beyond all doubts, the truth of His divine mission. His birth, life and death had been foretold by God through holy men called prophets several hundreds of years before their actual realisation and these things had been recorded in the books Taurat and Zabur (Old Testament) held sacred by the Jews long before the birth of Jesus, and honoured by Mahommed as God's revelations. In the actual birth, life and death of Jesus, everything that had been foretold about the promised Messiah or Redeemer, agree and correspond even to the minutest detail and therefore He is the promised Messiah. Such prerogatives cannot be found in any other religious

founder or reformer, whatever may be their other pretentions. Jesus proved the divinity of His mission by
working the greatest miracles of an astounding nature,
and besides raising several dead persons to life again,
He Himself though slain on a cross and buried, the
third day after his death rose again to life, in the most
wonderful manner, thus showing His almighty power,
and remained public in the world with His apostles and
disciples for forty days, after which in the presence of
a multitude of people, He with His might and power
ascended into heaven. Such wonderful perogatives
one cannot find in any other founder or reformer of any
other religion which alone should be enough to make
one follow the religion of Jesus in preference to any
other religion. All the incidents connected with the
birth, life and death of Jesus are recorded by four
different historians, who have written on the subject;
their manner of narrating the facts and the perfect
simplicity of their narratives prove the candour and
perfect veracity of the writers. These records we call
the four Gospels, or Ingil as Mahommed calls them.

The religion that has been revealed by God through
Jesus Christ as a guidance for mankind is all
holy, perfect and sublime and worthy of universal
admiration. If some followers of this holy religion are
found to be wicked and scandalous livers, it is not due
to this religion, but to their non-observance and abuse
of its teachings, and they are to be considered so
many unhappy black sheep that bring disgrace to the
fold.

Then, my dear friends, consider seriously; pray to
God to give you the grace of strength and fortitude;
shake off the unworthy yoke of Mahommed that has
been laid on your shoulders, and humbly follow the
great prophet Jesus, and following the true religion of
Jesus revealed to Him by heaven as Mahommed himself

testifies, save your immortal souls. This religion and the salutary means to save your soul you can find only in the Church which Christ founded and placed under the supreme guidance of Saint Peter and his successors to the end of time. This true Catholic religion was not propagated by the sword, as was Mahommed's religion; it defied the sword. During three hundred years under the pagan Emperors of Rome, there were innumerable bloody persecutions of Christians; philosophers with their keen sophistry and pagan priests with all their diabolical energy did their utmost to annihilate the religion of Christ; it withstood them all. It was founded on the rock of Saint Peter, against which the gates of hell shall never prevail, according to the promise of Christ. During subsequent ages it was assailed by various heresies under powerful leaders and by the formidable protestant reformation backed by several cruel monarchs; and even of late atheism, rationalism and freemasonry have done their utmost to destroy it.

All her enemies have gradually vanished away before her feet. Though robbed to a great extent of her earthly power, she has stood firm during all ages ever glorious, and will continue to stand as the only Teacher instituted by Jesus to teach mankind, the ground and pillar of truth. All other so called Christian sects are so many off-shoots that have fallen away from its trunk; like the many different sects that have sprung up in the pale of Mahommedanism, interpreting the sacred Scriptures as the latter do their Koran according to their own whims: and while only one of the Mahommedan sects can be the religion taught by Mahommed in his Koran, so the Holy Roman Catholic religion is the most primitive and the only true religion of Christ founded and placed under the supreme guidance of Saint Peter and his successors,

N

the Popes. It is the religion revealed by God as the one by which alone He desires to be worshipped. By following its doctrine and precepts one secures the eternal happiness of his soul. So courage, my dear friends, courage! be bold, and thus save your soul, and be eternally happy.

Your most sincere friend and well-wisher,

THE COMPILER.